Beyond Revolutions . . .

BEYOND REVOLUTIONS . . .
On Becoming a Cybernetic Epistemologist

June Di Salvo, Ph.D.

June Di Salvo, Ph.D

Foreword by Albert Ellis, Ph.D.

VANTAGE PRESS
New York / Los Angeles

FIRST EDITION

Published by Vantage Press, Inc.
516 West 34th Street, New York, New York 10001

Manufactured in the United States of America
ISBN: 0-533-08030-4

Library of Congress Catalog Card No.: 88-90163

To my professor
and chairperson of my advisory committee,
J. J. O'Brien,
A Libertarian and "Kindred Spirit."

Contents

Illustrations

Foreword

I have read many Ph. D. dissertations, some good and some bad, but few as interesting as June DiSalvo's *Beyond Revolutions . . . : On Becoming a Cybernetic Epistemologist*. It is truly a fascinating piece of work.

My liking for this book is all the more remarkable because I am hardly a devotee of Gregory Bateson and his kind of systems theory and therapy. He was a brilliant philosopher—but not necessarily an accurate one. His famous double-bind theory, while describing how people often think about themselves and others, implies that they *learn* to put themselves and others in double-binds, when the probability is high that they *innately* and *creatively* do so, with relatively little help from their parents and other influencers. As they largely *construct* their disturbed thoughts and feelings, they also *construct,* in the main, their own double-binds. So I think that Bateson was brilliant and profound—but, like Freud, a little *too* brilliant and therefore often unrealistic and inaccurate. He was sometimes too damned clever for his own good and for the field of family therapy.

Be that as it may, Dr. DiSalvo's study shows how people can remarkably change when faced with new and revolutionary ideas—whether or not these ideas are "true" or "false." Her subjects and herself were suddenly—and rather unpreparedly—confronted with a different cybernetic view of people and things, and they often suffered keenly in the process of absorbing and accepting this view; and some, of course, didn't really accept it. But in discovering this cybernetic outlook, they were forced to do something that humans often signally resist doing—think. Yes, think!

Dr. DiSalvo chronicles exactly what happened when this unusual process took place. Fortunately for my own theory of rational-emotive therapy (RET), her data show that her subjects not only were capable of making profound cognitive changes—which I have always contended people really can do— but that they concomitantly also experienced significant emotional and behavioral life changes. This, of course, is a central thesis of RET—that you largely (not completely) feel the way you think and that, interactionally and circularly, you tend to think the way you feel (Bernard, 1986; Ellis, 1962, 1973, 1988; Ellis & Dryden, 1987; Ellis & Harper, 1975; Walen, DiGiuseppe, & Wessler, 1980).

Even though scores of controlled studies have now shown that when disturbed people use RET to change their irrational beliefs they significantly tend to change their emotions and behaviors (DiGiuseppe, 1979; Ellis, 1979; Haaga & Davison, in press; McGovern & Silverman, 1984), people still vehemently tell me that this is *not* true and that the *only* way for therapy clients to change their disordered emotions is for them to stop thinking and to directly get in touch with their feelings and to engage in intense abreactive experiences. Maybe so. But the studies referred to above, and now Dr. DiSalvo's epistemological study, show otherwise. Create, somehow, a revolution in students' thinking and you will simultaneously tend to create, she notes, a revolution in their feelings and behaviors. And this second revolution will, apparently, interact with and importantly reaffect the first revolution!

I am happy that Dr. DiSalvo, working in an area that is somewhat removed from psychotherapy, has presented data that supports RET. Her study also makes a valuable philosophical and educational contribution that, I hope, will have widespread readership and influence. She is to be highly congratulated on this unique, and indeed evolutionary, effort.

Albert Ellis, Ph.D.
Executive Director
Institute for Rational-Emotive Therapy

References

Bernard, M. E. (1986). *Staying alive in an irrational world: Albert Ellis and rational-emotive therapy*. South Melbourne, Australia: Carlson/Macmillan.

DiGiuseppe, R. A., Miller, N. J., & Trexler, L. D. A review of rational-emotive psychotherapy outcome studies. In A. Ellis & J. M. Whiteley (Eds.), *Theoretical and empirical foundations of rational-emotive therapy* (pp. 218–235). Monterey, CA: Brooks/Cole.

Ellis, A. (1962). *Reason and emotion in psychotherapy*. Secaucus, NJ: Citadel Press.

Ellis, A. (1973). *Humanistic psychotherapy: The rational-emotive approach*. New York: McGraw-Hill.

Ellis, A. (1979). "Rational-emotive therapy: Research data that support the clinical and personality hypotheses of RET and other modes of behavior therapy." In A. Ellis & J. M. Whiteley (eds.), *Theoretical and empirical foundations of rational-emotive therapy* (pp. 101–173). Monterey, CA: Brooks/Cole.

Ellis, A. (1988). *How to stubbornly refuse to make yourself miserable about anything—yes, anything*. Secaucus, NJ: Lyle Stuart.

Ellis, A., & Dryden, W. (1987). *The practice of rational-emotive therapy*. New York: Springer.

Ellis, A., & Harper, R. A. (1975). *A new guide to rational living*. North Hollywood, CA: Wilshire Books.

Haaga, D. A., & Davison, G. C. (in press). "Outcome studies of rational-emotive therapy." In M. E. Bernard & R. Giuseppe (eds.), *Inside rational-emotive therapy*. Orlando, FL: Academic Press.

McGovern, T. E., & Silverman, M. S. (1984). "A review of outcome studies of rational-emotive therapy from 1977 to 1982." *Journal of Rational-Emotive Therapy, 2*(1), 7–18.

Walen, S. R., DiGiuseppe, R., & Wessler, R. L. (1980). *A practitioner's guide to rational-emotive therapy*. New York: Oxford.

Acknowledgments

The immediate acknowledgment for this book belongs to Albert Ellis, Ph.D., of Rational-Emotive Therapy (RET), who wrote its Foreword and inspired cognitive theory and its "ultimate fit" with *Beyond Revolutions: On Becoming a Cybernetic Epistemologist.* It is dedicated to the Chairperson of my dissertation advisory committee, J. J. O'Brien, Ph.D., but further I wish to acknowledge those who came to evolve as a "dynamite committee," which involved two others, A. E. Bender, Ph.D., and John DiTiberio, Ph.D. Ultimately, the "doctoral experience" involved professors Raphael Becvar, Ph.D., and Dorothy S. Becvar, Ph.D.; I am, by virtue of their gifted interactional approach to learning/teaching, a "Becvarian" to the core. Further, I am indebted to the theorists listed in the bibliography—particularly Bradford Keeney, Ph.D.; Catherine Bateson, Ph.D.; her father, Gregory Bateson; J. F. Rychlak; Thomas Kuhn; Lynn Segal, et. al; then to learned colleagues/respondents, who engaged in philosophical discourse, scheduled and unscheduled, and philosophical dialectic on cybernetics-and-beyond. Special thanks go to Edith Brayer, Ph.D. (ABD), for hours of listening and reading my first manuscript—and calling it "brilliant." Finally, thanks to Vantage Press, Inc., and its entire staff.

Introduction

> The deepest order of change that human beings are capable of demonstrating is epistemological change. . . . Understanding of cybernetic epistemology may completely alter one's habits of action . . . (Bradford Keeney, *Aesthetics of Change,* 1983.)

The major area of Ph.D. study of Individual, Marriage and Family Development and Therapy, at St. Louis University is a graduate level program of Counseling/Education that has been philosophically committed to the tenets of systems thinking. *Systems theory* favors cybernetic epistemology. *Cybernetics* focuses on the study of broad and chaotic feedback *patterns organizing,* micro and macro systems. *Epistemology* is a branch of philosophy that investigates the origins and nature of one's knowledge; "meta" to personality, it is *how we think know and decide.* Our philosophy of life. A cybernetic epistemology or "meta steering knowledge" is considered a learning level of the knowledge process, involving a profound leap or *change of world view.* It differs from earlier learning level changes in that it focuses on broad, complex patterns of the organization of cognitive process "about" or meta to "problem-solving" and "self" psychology.

In a review of the literature—since the scattered patterns seemed overwhelming for the focus of the chaotic experience of change of world view—organizing concepts fit well into frames constructed as *traditional, residual,* and *emergent.* The *traditional frame* considers key meta-assumptions connected to the "lingering" 17th-century world views of Locke and Kant; traditional views present an early pattern of conflict. The *residual frame* portrays how the earlier persistent pattern of *conflict dynamics* (Revolutions) has infiltrated and settled in the 20th century. Dominant conflict (Revolution) dynamics persist as THE pattern and prescribed process, for ANY AND ALL profound sociocultural, economic, political, religious, etcs., CHANGE. In the *residual frame* the circular pattern of organization of REVOLUTIONS AS CHANGE, as paradigm shift, is considered and graphically illustrated. It is in an *emergent frame* that the vision of higher level learning change—as experiential process—that the patterns of cognitive dissonance and what I call *"cybernetic shock"* is chronicled and graphically mapped. Heuristic patterns connect a theme of change of world view which elucidates the higher level learning change moving *BEYOND REVOLUTIONS: OR BECOMING A CYBERNETIC EPISTEMOLOGIST*. Various patterns of cybernetic epistemology, invented and taken from the literature, present complex theories that overarch the pattern of conflict of traditional/residual-Revolutionary frames. Reframed as *emergent-and-beyond,* these key complex constructs of the past decade, of leading scientists/scholars of the field of cybernetics and related sciences, are considered, rehearsed and illustrated as involving connecting patterns.

"Un-methodological" heuristic inquiry is experientially narrated and used as the meta-pattern of organization throughout this study and re-search. Heuristic intentions involve formulating a pattern of questions from/for study and review of literature, meant to illuminate the theme of change of world view. Heuristics frees up creative cognitive process thereby inspiring personally meaningful experiences and leaps of intellect and emotions. This book neither reaches for conclusions nor seeks to "problem-solve," forthwith denying its readers that personally, profoundly fulfilling experience of inventing a new world view. To chronicle this, graduate students ($N = 7$ of $n = 67$) involved in the process of becoming cybernetic epistemologists were interviewed. The expressed verbal content (EVC) of graduate student responses, audiotaped verbatim transcriptions (chapter 4), "match" and illuminate those patterns that connect becoming cybernetic epistemologists to the theme of change of world view—Beyond Revolutions as change. . . .

Personal Pro-Log to "Knowing" a Cybernetic Epistemology: Learning *about* Learning

> ". . . there is a view of the world that rests entirely on paradox. The news that epistemologists . . . bring us is that all living and mental process involves *recursion, self-reference, and paradox.* This perspective is the world of cybernetics and cybernetics of cybernetics" (Keeney, 1983, p. 56).

For the spring semester of 1986 I enrolled in one of the final required courses for study in Ph.D. graduate education. Catalogued as Advanced Individual, Marriage & Family Therapy (ED 145-665-01), there was *no* reference to the course content being of a "philosophical nature." I had the habit of purchasing textbooks before the first class meeting, so my initial shock was finding *seven* books—at a cost of $135 and designated as "required reading"—on topics seemingly unrelated to psychotherapy/counseling. Incredulous as it seemed (one book every two weeks for the fourteen weeks, and then FINALS), the course description revealed that each student would function as "discussion leader" for one week and one book—as sort of "guest professor,"—and grades would be determined by this function and ensuing class participation, as well as a written (ungraded and "limited" to five typewritten pages per assignment) reaction or experiential log, which was to be handed in every third week throughout the semester.

Nearly everyone has memories of significant courses, teachers, books, articles, authors, encounters, et cetera, that they label as "turning points" in their lives. This course—the readings, discussions, the presentations, the professor—was more of a "LAUNCHING SITE," for the becoming process, topic, and writing of this book, adapted from my Ph.D. dissertation (the Pro-Log *is not* part of my formal dissertation). Reading the following reaction log I (and the reader) can pick up the early stirring of ideas and cybernetic connections that vibrated, perturbed re-construction, and launched epistemological change of my world view. The following experiential log was "rediscovered" and included as "evidence" to "acknowledge that we have always been cybernetic epistemologists; the *trick is in knowing*. It turns out that THE

PH.D . . . IS THE PROCESS OF BECOMING PH.D.! (The "magnificent 7" texts for this course are stared in the bibliography.)

Reaction Log

*Note: Comments in brackets are those of Dorothy Stroh-Becvar, Ph.D. [D.S.B], the professor teaching the course.

Weeks 1, 2 and 3, (Reading Assignment: Bronowski's *The Origins of Knowledge and Imagination,* 1978).

1st Class meeting: *SEVEN*—count 'em again—seven—books (texts) on PHILOSOPHY! The subject itself has a way of sending "shivers" up and down my spine. "The study of the truths and principles of being, knowledge, or conduct." I ask myself, "Have I come this far?" My vision (Idealism) of a leisurely semi-sabbatical time to integrate concepts fades with the enormity of the tasks. I don't think it clicked with me what is involved in the attainment of a Ph.D. until now! Am I so blind to the obvious that is means what it says: *Doctorate in Philosophy* . . . Have I "bitten off more than I can chew" (?)—and I fall back to the metaphorical stance of "How do you eat an elephant standing in the road?" "One bite at a time!" (of course.)

I am most impressed with the intelligence and ability to articulate concepts—of those around me; two or three of these have been in previous classes. Marlena "says it all" and at times leaves me breathless, "lost" with her abilities to articulate difficult philosphical matters. Howard, I do not know, but seems a delightful, extremely bright addition. Nina I have worked with professionally, and I envy her youthful yet mature depth of knowledge and experience. Andrew and I have shared the learning process and have a rapport something like "East meets West," the exchange is enjoyable. Nancy, while not as verbal as the others, impresses me with her creative soft-spoken "clout." Vivian, Barb, Kathy and Pris are new to me—as is Dorothy S. Becvar, Ph.D.! It was a pleasant surprise to me—I had expected "the other" Dr. Becvar! I had hoped to "travel a path of learning" with you (Dorothy)—this one seems difficult—your assurance that *it will* come together is encouraging. I am encouraged enough to "tackle" my first "bite" of the elephant in the road and "taste" Bronowski's (1978) *The Origins of Knowledge and Imagination*—TONIGHT!

Next A.M.: Maybe it was something I *ate* last night! Or was it the opening mini-lecture on Martin Luther King, Jr., or the solution to the

9 dot puzzle of *Change* (1974)? It could have been what at first seemed like a "tough" morsel—the first 2 chapters of the "Silliman Lectures . . . of *Origins*." I remember reading on, very late—I crawled into bed and recall "visual purple's" appearance in the brief moments before I fell asleep I searched for some sort of pattern; it was wispy—then it covered the entire field of my closed-lids vision, and was accompanied by sounds of systems, within myself.

I remember dreams infrequently. Perhaps that's why I tend to consider their symbolism incredible; wide open to interpretations. In REM sleep our "form" is in a state called paralysis. Perhaps the state is necessary for other forms to be activated. In my dream I have *taken something that doesn't belong to me.* (YET?) It takes a *very long time* and a lot of *wrong turns* to discover the *way back,* to return it. It gets *very late* and I am wondering if I should just *give up*—but I want so to return it before it is missed. "It" is not at all clear or describable until context is available. I am on the street or in the corridors of a huge institution (Oxford?)—it is another time, possibly the 19th century. My surroundings are London-like and I'm aware of the dangers for a woman alone—here and now. I dart in and out of the institution—loaded with strange baggage, my unzipped shoulderbag, a portable TV, a cassette recorder, and a cloth drawstring bag—filled with oranges (?) and dull pointed objects sticking out of the bag, not coming through, but making it hard to maneuver. I feel I am going in the right direction but it is getting later and later. I have darted into the institution, and after following a long corridor it opens suddenly into a large high-ceilinged room with a bar on the far side. A few sleazy looking inebriated people and a barman are there. Coming up behind me—and then they are alongside me—are three threatening gowned, hooded forms. The big one on my right is trying to control my path and pushing me bodily toward the two on my left, one of whom is eeriely drawing up a syringe I'm afraid is meant for me! As I glance back I notice my handbag is unzipped—but my hands are full. I have made it this far on my own—but now I NEED HELP! As they close in—I realize no one is aware of my plight unless I open my mouth —a scream just doesn't seem appropriate . . . So I YELL "NO! STOP! PRESIDENT REAGAN WILL GET YOU!!!" Then I woke with a marvelous sense of relief! This "eye-opening" (both/and) experience stimulated my appetite for more of Bronowski's fare. I "made" breakfast, lunch, dinner, and a late-night snack of "*Origins.*" Turned down corners of pages, margin notes, underlined passages, expanded and connected "science and art" as creative activities. Experiencing, with this author, the interconnectedness of things and actions; the partial-ity of view (there's always more than meets the eye); the likeness in diversity; how language, a form of symbols invented, or perhaps more accurately evolved, is subject to interpretation by foresight, prolongation of reference, internalization, stratification and reconstitution; how one "cannot make a single general statement about anything in the world which really is wholly delimited, wholly unambiguous, and divides the world into two pieces." Bronowski helps to "heal" the tendency to split things and actions in order to "understand, predict, and control our worlds,"—in splitting we tend to forego connectedness and believe we have discovered the truth.

2nd Class meeting: I had "consumed" a small portion (1/7) of the elephant standing in the path. This meeting served to stimulate the "digestive" process and allow the expression and exchange of the experience of Bronowski. [Nice metaphor! D.S.B.] (I have the feeling that this might be an appetizer—and yet, it maybe of the gourmet "Lite" variety—satisfying, which makes one come back for more.) The introduction of the basic assumptions underlying the Kantian world view (and Lockean) "fits" well with the fare. Perhaps my dream—was a metaphor—(My bias!) the beginning of science—"something deeper than words." Being able to share it with a professional "cuddle group" calms the "crazies" when self-talk centers around creative leaps and change [Whitaker would like this . . . D.S.B.]. Einstein put it in these words, "Great spirits have always encountered violent opposition from mediocre minds." I had this quote in mind when I spoke of the feelings of compulsion to speak out, write about the knowledge and imagination contained within my particular life "banquet."

Thru an *inductive* process and *dialectic* mode we catch glimpses of our own and others' *epistemology*. (A bit awkward, but the language of philosophy, while not foreign to me, has not fit the context of my experiences til now. With time I'll do better.) On to Khun (1962, 1970), and *The Structure of Scientific Revolutions!*

Week 3—We cannot leave Bronowski behind—"Evolution is built up by the perpetuation of errors." *Structure* brings this home *tautologically*. To me Kuhn suffers the fate of following the "tantalizing appetizer," a priori—in the aesthetics of Bronowski. In a way I see Kuhn trying to bridge the gap between "old and new" world views (Locke and Kant, 17th & 18th century, respectfully). [Agreed. D.S.B.] His accounts of the experience of scientists—(see the Einstein quote earlier) and the lag between discovery/invention and acceptance ruins one's "craving" for this "ethnic" traditional fare. One other thing keeps coming to mind: Successful revolutions, historically, have been backed by *those in power* . . . those that have failed lacked this element. [This sounds a bit linear: $ = power-success. D.S.B.]. If those in power (this usually means funds or the acquisition of) are in the position of losing power, it makes no difference what the masses feel or need. [And power can be defined in many ways. D.S.B.] If the masses can persuade those in power that it is to their benefit (those in power) for them to revolt—the necessary backing for successful "object level" revolution has been secured. The level "meta" remains the same. Whew! I have stretched the "limits" of 5 pages—and find myself finishing the "soup"—which seemed more a "stew," heavy and filled with a variety of overly cooked, hard to identify ingredients, seasoned with unfamiliar spices which make it "hot" but seem cold. Five "courses" to go and I feel full—yet unsatisfied. The conversation (dialectic) is much more stimulating that I at first anticipated and express—just three short weeks ago.

[I hope each course will give some new tastes to stimulate your palate as well as some old ones which satisfy your appetite. Excellent log. D.S.B.]

Reaction Log

Advanced Individual, Marriage & Family Therapy
ED 145-665-01
Weeks 4 & 5 (Assignment: Kuhn's; *The Structure of Scientific Revolutions* 1962, 1970).

I'm trying to determine when it happened . . . Second order change can occur imperceptably—then it can occur like a bolt-from-the-blue. As I look back, as an undergrad, I thought instructors and students sounded pretentious and unclear when they refered to particular books by author's name only. My bias! I guess it caught on in my training in nursing. "Brunner" was the wordname—for *The Textbook of Medical-Surgical Nursing (1980);* there was a co-author, but his/her name was never connected. We spoke in a "code" that we all understood in the profession. I thought of it as the bible of nursing.

Then, at the Masters level in Social Work, and a bachelors in psychology, books and authors seemed to "compound semi-anually." My resistance added to my confusion. I found myself shuffling through piles of books—in and outside of class—trying to "crack the code." Another thing "bothers" me is the "disappearance" of *symbolic interactionsim* and *conflict theory;* [They haven't disappeared. D.S.B.] the two theories coveted by the School of Social Work! Where have they gone? [Sociology. D.S.B.] Honestly, I had never heard of—(I hate to admit it)—this twosome before Social Work, or since. Don't ask me the authors! All I remember is something about the Chicago and Iowa schools and Marx—and many, many axioms! [Berger and Hackman. D.S.B.]

I think—I have finally reached the limit of my resistance! I now speak and understand "in code (encode?)!" I caught myself doing this piecemeal in the early classes of doctoral studies in my classes with Ray (Becvar, Ph.D.) and Jarad (Balmar, Ph.D.) *This* class has me speaking the language of the profession like a pro! The "code" immediately brings symbols to my mind—along with the feeling "I know much more than I think I know." I love it! Bronowski, Kuhn, and Hampden-Turner (is only one author!), are fertile symbols that stimulate a far-away look in my eyes and an altered state hard for me to conceptualize. A second or third meaning of one of the philosopy words in the list of the language "of" may work—"An electromotive force in a neighboring body without contact;" *Induction?* (Literally the process of reasoning from specific to general.) A bolt from the blue. This is not a "use a new word in a sentence exercise," but "*heuristic*" fits the process (encourage the student to discover for himself). I can hardly wait to add "code names: " Bateson, Briggs & Peat, Ferguson, and Hesse, to a priori ontological views. (Am I able to synthesize the state of confusion necessary to communicate how best I manifest learning & growth?) I catch myself, these days, saying, "Title? Who's the *author?*" [And it will be important to be able to cite source, for your exams. D.S.B.]

Class discussion: Kuhn's *The Structure of Scientific Revolutions* proved to be a "tough morsel" to digest. One feels breathless & speechless after wrestling with "simple" understanding. The discussion leader (Marlena) lived up to my expectation voiced earlier. She covered and stretched our sense of imagination and knowledge with the overlay of philosophical terms. The "mix" and "texture" of the ingredients was in fine taste. I envy her ability to "art-iculate" difficult concepts and processes. The covert feud between 16th century empiricists and 17th century dialectics rambles on. With the Lockean world view—which fits paradigms into an agreed upon body of knowledge—keeping a "deep hold on scientific minds;" forcing nature into conceptual boxes. Normal science is not aimed at "new" phenomena. I'd like to suggest that the complexity of the world has increased since the 16th century, (and the 17th), as has the agreed upon body of knowledge. I keep thinking how complex systems move toward their own destruction. . . . [What is the logical complement of destruction? D.S.B.]

Questions & puzzle-solving of "mega-problems" of peace, cancer, and crime have necessarily been delegated to their own "scientific communities" of politics, medicine and legal systems. Could it be that there is a connection between this phenomena and normal science—in the history of revolutions, traditional paradigms are not abandoned with falsity—"this would involve relenquishing whole *structures* . . . of organized (& *organizations*) of knowledge. There might be a connection between "dirty politics," "orphan drugs" and legal curruption. Kuhn inspired this personal thought with his reference to the educational system's "laundered to fit" texts used in the induction process (errors compounded upon errors, ad-infinitum—Bronowski-like). The switch to natural science's dialectic may keep the "body" stable—a dyad is by nature unstable—in its *complimentary* or symmetry . . . Is this crazy? *What about a thearapeutic triangulation of the cybernetic world view* —or is that where we're going? Whew! [Good question. D.S.B.] [Author's note (6/1988): In this log entry I spelled complimentary, as in insincere or dubious compliments . . . and had instituted the path to learning level III and cybernetic epistemology—my resolution of meta-double-bind!]

Marlena quoted G. Spencer Brown, "We draw boundries, we shuffle the cards—we make the distinctions." I liked that. And—"Reorganization—through discovery is imagination." (Bronowski). Right on!

Class question: As I reread "Postscript—1969" of Kuhn's 2nd enlarged edition of *Revolutions*(1962, 1970)—these points stood out:

1) On fundamentals his viewpoint is very nearly unchanged.
2) He now re-cognizes aspects of its initial formulation that create gratuitous difficulties and misunderstandings.
3) *Some* of these misunderstandings have been his own.
4) Their elimination enables him to gain ground that should provide the basis for new version of this book.

He then ends with an indication that there is "likeness in diversity" of developed scientific processes (schools):

1) the scarcity of competing schools (sets it apart)
2) the members of the community are the only audiences & judges
3) Scientific education is puzzle solving as goals
4) The value system which the group deploys in crisis & decision. (sets it apart)

Question: Hampden-Turner helped me with this formulation: Has the structure of the organization of scientific discovery and invention taken on the characteristics of a rigidly closed system—and taken on many of the often maligned bureaucracy traits it paradoxically abhors?

Reaction Log

Advanced Individual, Marriage & Family Therapy ED 145-665-01 Weeks 6, 7 & 8 (*Class presentation* on Assigned reading: *Maps of the Mind,* Hampden-Turner, 1981)

I have just devoured the "main course" of the colossal gourmet meal—I consumed it as slowly as was possible for me . . . Maps of the Mind (MOM), by C. Hampden-Turner (1981) left me feeling stuffed with bits and pieces—chunks of information which slipped thru the cracks and somehow came out in coherent form. I plan to include my "preparatory" and wrapup remarks as "guest professor" as part of this course log. It will then not be "lost" among the "Q" cards I have restuffed in the book. (Note: the following assignment as co–discussion leader.)

Process & Procedure: Introductory remarks (after Nancy's experiential exercise of Guided Imagry of Mind Mapping)

"Now—since thru Imagery—we have connected our right brain functions—we move on. First, if you haven't completed reading the book do! Nancy and I can't wait to see the documentary movie version. . . . Since one of us has already "soloed," as discussion leader and pairs of us are scheduled to direct these dialectics—I thought it might be interesting to describe how Nancy and I arrived at this point—it occurred to me right after I had first read thru MOM—and was on my way to the lavatory, before meeting here with Nancy. I would have had the class, through discussion and concensus of scientific opinion—construct a composite . . . our own ORIGINAL MAP—and vote on a synthesis.

I LIKED Nancy's creative experiential guided Imagery better—The one we have just completed, mapping our own minds. It "fits."

Next, and don't ask me why now—I'll explain later at the wrapup—I proposed that we use the Inductive process of Emanuel Kant's World View as a kind of meta-theoretical outline—to demonstrate how select theory is related in these ways. Nancy liked this too.

Finally, and not by a toss of the coin, but thru scholarly discourse we decided who would like to "do" which order of categorical level; we arrived at an ODD-even level number split. I get the ODDS—which I find significant—ODD THINGS HAVE BEEN GOING ON IN MY MIND EVER SINCE! So—

After this, Nancy will do an Introduction to Maps, and I will follow with the first (odd) level to lead off discussion of these. Nancy will follow that with the even levels and so on—thru the nine levels we hope!

Since we recognize the "Irreversibility of Time" we have had to limit each level discussion time. One of our props is a timer. [A nice touch—tacky, but nice. D.S.B.] Subjective reactions/discussion will have to beat the clock—so to speak.

We have limited our remarks too—to start discussions of specific maps. If it fits we have alloted time after the wrap-up. And, then there is additional time next class for further discussion. (Take it away Nancy . . .)"

WRAP-UP

During the process & procedure portion of this presentation—I promised to explain—the *choice* Nancy & I made—using Kantian World View & the inductive process.

During preparation for this discussion—I was "haunted" by some "thing in the bushes," which looked like the Uroborus—the mythical snake that devours its tail. Its beginnings elude me. (Equifinality)

Then, I remembered a reference to sociologist Max Weber mentioned back in Map 7, Protestantism, Scientism, Capitalism, . . . Around the turn of this century Weber indulged in what he called "thought experiments." We might well call it brainstorming today. He practiced considering "comical, bizarre, irrational, absurd social arrangements in an attempt to shed light" on macro-problems. The one I remember best, from Social Work Values & Ethics was: "What if—women are equal?"

My own thought experiments went something like this: What if—Nancy & I had not agreed on a SPLIT, odd-even catagorical levels of this class presentation/discussion? The process might have turned out chaotic & less than coherent—much like the movie reviews on TV—with each interrupting & disagreeing—as we cast "Yeh" or "Ney" votes for some of the "oldies but goodies," and panned the new "flicks."

Or, Nancy could say a word, then me, then her, then me until time and/or (both-and) patience ran out—accompanied by all class members.

What I am trying to describe is how SPLITTING has negative connotation—only if WHOLE is not seen as its complementary [author 1988 note: spelling] opposite—& vise versa. IT IS ECOLOGICALLY IMPORTANT TO PRESERVE THIS THOUGHT—(&Nancy's & my sanity)—during these last remarks.

The evaluation of complimentarity [author's 1988 note: spelling] of opposites is as old as—going out on a limb—Christianity? Yes? No? Maybe? Both-and . . . Or was it when humans first discovered they could act upon the environment—and it looked, sounded, felt, tasted, smelled, or rolled, better. Better than when they waited around for things to happen—and then they reacted.

Or was value expressed in a pre-language mode—much as an infant stops its squalling & sleeppppppps—as a measure & evaluation of the quality and quantity of food, warmth and love received & given?

OR, billions of years ago—one Sunday afternoon—did Neanderthal Man look at and say to Neanderthal Woman: "BAD!" when he bit into the dinosaur roast she had charred in the too hot fire. She probably might have replied: "GOOD!—It's well-done! AND what's more—YOU can do the damn Bar-B-Q from now on!" Perhaps the first "conflicting world views."

I have a confession to make—when Dorothy supplied us—and it's in our notes—with the two world views of Kant & John Locke, she did give us Kant's first. Right? She *did not* label or evaluate them in any way—other than giving (listing) Kant's first. How many of you did what Nancy & I did? We immediately set them up as *opposite & conflicting World Views*. And, of course we thought that Kant's was preferred because it was *presented first*—of course—along with a lot of other "necessary & sufficient" reasons.

Initially I intended to present Kant as the "Good Guy," and Locke as BAAAD! Either/or. After all wasn't it Lockean World View that had gotten us in the mess-up Bronowski, Kuhn, & HT describe? And, his way obviously isn't working perfectly, so try the opposite! My reasoning was all "Locke-d" into linear—cause/effect, Cartesian Dualism. Still, something didn't seem quite right.

So, I re-read & studied in detail all the ODD levels I've presented for our learned discussions. I find I have arrived at yet another obvious bias (To which Nancy had agreed!)—Kantian & Lockean World Views are complimentary (1988—note: D.S.B. "corrected my spelling of complimentary") opposites at the OBJECT LEVEL—and so are the *same* at a meta-level; nested & dovetailed they are synergistic & ecologically both-and.

Two weeks ago, when I came into class late - and Marlena had these two headings on the board, "Kant - Locke"—I had the feeling black poetess Ntozake Shange laments: "Somebody almost walked off with all my stuff." I wondered then where to go with Kant & Locke. . . . I was in real danger of throwing the baby out with the bathwater.

"The Key to the Solution" jumped out at me from my scribbled notes—as most scientific breakthroughs do! Reciprocity lies at the meta-level—above the object level—(OK, Dorothy?) I began to see the "likeness in diversity."

And—is it possible that the best description of the elusive (Best) "Truth" lies at the intersect—juxtapositioned at both-and . . . of these 16th & 17th Century World Views? At the sigmoid curve, as in the interpretation of Jonas Salk Map 46? (Maps of the Mind)

PRO-LOG MAP 61

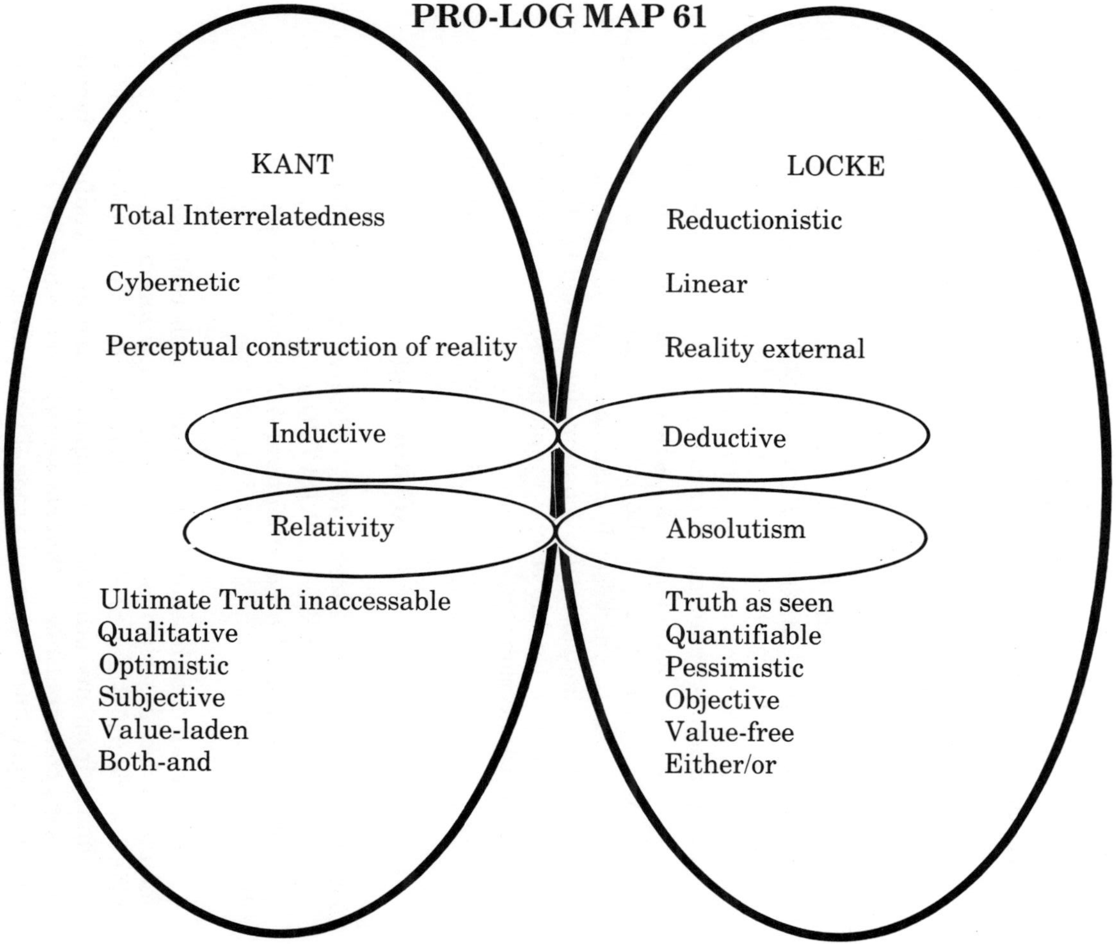

Then, I remembered Ray (Becvar, Ph.D.), saying a number of times: "Answers are contained in the questions asked." I began connecting the two elements in the views with lazy-eight recursive forms. . . .

I fondly, perhaps grandiosely, present this as MAP 61, an ODD one—as a meta-world view. Dare we name it? DiSalvo's Immaculate Deception? The Ravings of "an almost imperfect Theorist!" [Sounds good to me! D.S.B.]

It may be unnecessary, but in case my "Map 61" "IS" the "territory," and/or has appeared elsewhere in print—I feel it ethically necessary to say: That for this brief moment in time, it is original & MINE—ALL MINE—and not a reproduction!

I conclude with the thought (and I'm not sure at this point if its original or I read it somewhere)—That if we split these World Views—we make the broken halves into idols. An ecological synergy of values (world views) optimizes the elements.

Education is balanced precariously between catastrophy of split. The choice is not between poles - it lies ecologically in both-and.

Now we will "uncover the inner workings of this model of the Mind. . . . (plastic model of human skull) By now the "connections" can be made—heuristically. (content for Thought) (Puzzle-making, Chinese Fortune Cookie & one round ballon—no two exactly alike.) Make the connections?

[Very well done, June. (A+) D.S.B.]

Reaction Log

Advanced Individual, Marriage & Family Therapy ED 145-665-01
Weeks 9 & 10—*"BASKING IN BATSON - and 'OTHER' AFFAIRS"*
(Assigned reading: *Mind and Nature. A Necessary Unity,* G. Bateson, 1979)

It was an intellectual "high" that I wish could last forever-the feeling defied description. The mental stimulation surrounding the effort of "doing" *Maps of the Mind* for/with the group; having Todd (a classmate from my other class), approach me and "confide" how he enjoys my contributions to that class—my "wise remarks" have "made" the class very interesting and thought-provoking for him. And often, I exchanged, I've felt like what I have to say is uninteresting & uneventful for most—that his telling me was one of the nicest things I've experienced in a while/and thanks for the unsolicited indorsement and encouragement! Then Howard & I talked on the way to class, he said that he'd heard that he's "missed" a "terrific" presentation—the word gets around, I guess—that's nice. (1988; My grade? A+) "Strokes" like this are something I've been missing for a lot of my life. I do this with others—but it seems . . . perhaps, it's the case of putting forth special effort—and having someone notice. Then, following that high, came the special private experience of "being ONE, with Batson." When I finished his book I had the feeling that I wanted to experience it in the same way—again and again. I had the feeling that he and I saw, heard, felt, smelled(?) and tasted "life"-*Mind & Nature (1979)*—in the same ways, at different times and in different places. My experiences are not as scholarly, nor as well documented, nor as well thought out, etc., etc., as his. Yet, for the time I was reading his work for the first time WE WERE ONE! [Lovely! D.S.B.] Was it a case of "a priori" existence? Again I'm beginning to "sound" rather grandiose. "So full" of the "entre" of Hampden-Turner's "Maps"—I was looking forward to a refreshing light "sorbet" when the "waiter" comes up with a delectable, different, new dish—one I "must just taste" or the "chef" will be distressed. . . . I think it was like a wonderfully lite pasta—the kind you expect to make it necessary to "loosen any restraining garment." I sat back, contemplated the "serving," reluctantly picked up the proper utensil, and "twirled" it round before taking the first bite. I was filled—from the start—with aesthetics—I have *never* experienced —anything like it before. . . . How else can I describe (sticking with the metaphor of devouring an elephant!)? (Am I making *you* hungry?) I finished every morsel. And I say, "My compliments to the Chef!" It did make it necessary for me to sit back again—and "bask in Bateson" for a while longer. I simply could not get into anything else for a time. One cannot "consume" a meal like this quickly. [And everyone eats at their own pace. D.S.B.]

Cathy and Barbara had their own creative highs too (as guest professors). They seemed to experience the process as Nancy & I had. I'm really glad "I read the book before seeing the play!" The whole thing made so much more sense. And, they were making connections with our connections. Am I being grandiose again? Or did I hear my name in the "credits?" Barbara did say, did she not(?) that my "Map 61, DiSalvo's Magnificent Deception—The Ravings of an Almost Imperfect Theorist!" was a primary inspiration for their "binocular" vision thought processes. Was the recursive, complimentary opposite conceptualization of Kantian and Lockean world views the kind of "stuff" theories are made of?

I have to admit, to the "fickleness" of "having these kinds of experiences" with other authors/theorists. It has *never* [I'm very glad to hear that. D.S.B.] come down to either/or is "the one" for me. I got down to thinking about this after our discourse . . . the way I would describe "me," is as a "BOTH—AND kind of "gal." Maybe this is contrary to what is demanded by societal institutions . . . NO MAYBES—IT IS! It has always been "which is the right one." A better word would be *changeableness* (change-ableness, I like that!) And, before you are tempted to "write in," the compl*i*mentary opposite is stability (smile, giggle, they should have one of those smilely faces on typewriters). [Some do! D.S.B.]—Flexibility is my next try—maybe the "highs" will not be soo high that it hurts to come down to, where "normalacy" seems low. . . . Falling within the MEAN—interestingly enough has complimentary (spelling note) opposites like: inferior, superior, *beginning,* and *end.*

"Briggs & Peat" (1984) is next on the menu—strange sounding—I wonder how it will "sit" after "5 courses." [How indeed . . . D.S.B.]

[Very nice log. Your enthusiasm is infectious. D.S.B.]

(OVER?) Reaction Log

v. June DiSalvo ED 145-665-01 Weeks 11 & 12 (Assigned reading: *Looking Glass Universe,* 1984, Briggs & Peat)

"Somehow it seems to fill my head with ideas only I don't exactly know what they are." (Carroll, 1865)" . . . like vague forms emerging out of the mist." (Briggs & Peat, 1984 p. 270) It is five-&-a-half minutes 'till Sunday and I have finished *Looking Glass Universe, (1984) AND* reading the *The Annotated Alice* (Gardner, 1960)—*in part.* Bohr is quoted (p. 272) as thinking up all the "crazy ideas he could on Mondays, Wednesdays, and Fridays"—and on Tuesdays, Thursdays, and Saturdays "try to disprove them." This was no help! It's Sunday now—I'll try *both—and.* (I will be away, most likely, when you read this—and we will have completed our class dialectics on the subject of the *Looking Glass Universe,* and I really can't say if I can bring up *THIS* reaction in class—I don't yet know where it "fits" and/or misfits . . .)

When I read the passage from Lewis Carroll's *Through the Looking Glass,* I felt a "void" existed in my education as a child (and of course—it followed as and adult Grad Student!) I mentioned in class that "Fairy Tales" were "absent" as a part of my growth and development. Occasionally, I felt deprived—and guilty—at not experiencing this seemingly universal literary medium, and/or reading them to my own (four) children. Reading it I felt somehow "left out" of "the conspiracy." I found the passage & the book frightening, absurd, almost obscene in the light of present knowledge concerning physical, sexual, & emotional abuse of children. There are very few books I read that I can honestly say "I almost wish I hadn't come across it." Andrew had generously offered his borrowed from the University copy, and I "had" to fill that void—to gain a greater understanding of the "emerging science of wholeness." I read their book (B & P) first—and then counted on the *ORIGINAL SOURCE* to complete the "rosy picture," after I'd read a good part of the tale—I began to feel "quezzy" about the "sorbet" (of the gourmet fare presented) . . . it tasted delectable, rich and yet the proper "following" after the other (4) "courses." Perhaps it was something on/in the container it came in. That's the way it is sometimes—with an "upset"—you never find out the CAUSE. I searched the index and the title pages of Briggs & Peat for reference to Carroll's "classic." I COULD NOT FIND ONE! It is small consolation—but I *hope* they have never read the Carroll work in its entirety—for me it cast a bleak shadow on theirs.

I asked Andrew, at the conference this weekend, if he had read the Introduction to "Alice"—which, since this annotation was done in 1960, "reveals" the author as . . . "neurotic" & "the hobby that aroused his greatest joys—was entertaining little girls." He is quoted, "I am fond of children (his quote!) except boys." "He sketched or photographed them in the nude, with the mother's permission, (what about Dad's?) of course." " . . . he carried a supply of safety pins for pinning up the skirts of little girls . . . never ceased looking for such a child (perfection). He became adept at meeting little girls in railway carriages and on public beaches. A black bag that he always took with him on these trips contained wire puzzles and other unusual gifts to stimulate their interest." OF COURSE this edition exonerates—Carroll of the "dirty old man" of fairytales image (my bias!) (p 13). "There is no indication that Carroll was conscious of anything but the purest innocence in his relations with little girls." And, "The thing that distinguishes Carroll from other writers who lived sexless lives (Thoreau, Henry James . . .) and from writers who were strongly drawn to little girls (Poe, Ernest Dowson . . .) was his curious combination, almost unique in literary history, of complete sexual innocence with a passion that can only be described as thoroughly heterosexual." MY IMPLICATE ORDER OF FREQUENCY, in this case, is making my "gut" *feel* sicker and sicker. It is getting harder and harder to contain . . . The implications are so profound! It only surfaced in the past decade that the prevalence of just this kind of abuse has come to light! And Victorian Times seems to have been a "hot bed" of incest and "other" victimization of children (mostly females). The "thing" most sickening is the veneration of this (and other) literary "classics." And the fact that countless numbers of children have read and been "read to" from them! It is no further consolation to me, at this time, to feel personally "unvictimized," or unabused, at not having "experienced" much of this literary form! I feel ANGRY and no better at having "vented my spleen" on paper. It's best I crawl into bed and "thank my lucky stars," some well-meaning adult was not around to read me a fairy tale "classic" of this sort . . .

PS—Have you had the chance to read *Assault on the Truth* (Masson, 1984)? I'll loan it to you, if you think I haven't "over-reacted" to this off the schedule reading! It is about Freud's "suppression of" just this kind of abuse in his (Victorian) time . . . (1890)

PSS—I want to say "tell me it isn't true . . . "—that Briggs & Peat have *ever* read or known the "stuff" of "Alice." [I'm sure they have. D.S.B.]

PSSS—I'm having "desert & coffee" on the ship—*The Conspiracy* & *The Glass Bead Game* may settle me—*some.*

(I think I may have heard a "lecherous" laugh last night when I went to bed & turned off the lights. Did it come over the centuries?) [Perhaps . . . D.S.B.]

[I think you are entitled to your reactions/overreactions whatever they are . . . I would be careful however not to confound the intentions of one author with those of another, especially when the only thing borrowed may have been a useful metaphor. However, if the context of the metaphor is distasteful to you, it is bound to flavor the taste of the dish prepared with it. D.S.B.]

[Very nice log. Have a wonderful trip! D.S.B.]

Returning—Reaction Log

ED145-665-01
FINAL LOG Weeks 13, 14 & 15 (Missed class reading: *The Aquarian Conspiracy,* Ferguson, (1980) (Final reading: *Magister Ludi: The Glass Bead Game,* Hesse 1969)

"I CAN'T BELIEVE! I ATE THE *WHOLE* THING! The seven course gourmet fare set forth for "consummation," has come to its timely close. I sampled half of "desert" (Ferguson's "Conspiracy") in a state of confusion and vertigo which I attributed to my idiosyncratic extreme sensitivity to things that move sideways as they go up and down or in circles—without detectable rhythm/harmony. I leave street-cars and carnival rides in an "upset" bilious state. I "saved" Howard's and Pris's tape until the inner-frequencies returned to their previous state—so I could "tune-in and turn-on" and CONSPIRE! They tried to "reach" me—over the waves—how were they to know that context was jamming the circuits! (I am reminded of the KY98 broadcast and Fisch's video-taped session at the "Inn.") Yet, in 3 or 4 days I felt "transformed"—balance/imbalance restored. (Jet-lag/cruise ship vertigo)

Coffee! That did help. Incidentally, I also seem to experience a paradoxical reaction to this substance. Coffee (& Hesse's first 250 pages of *The Glass Bead Game*—the last of seven books) puts me to sleep; while alcoholic beverages stimulate and tend to prevent rest. "The Game" is many things to many people—and EVERYTHING to some. . . . An old cliche: "It's not whether you win or lose, but how you play . . . " and I'll add, and in what *context*—makes ALL the difference. I've never liked games—I usually (no always) lose—so I'm biased. Bridge and some Trivial Pursuit I find sociable. I've said, "There's not a competitive bone in my body;" and I enjoy and play a *fair* game of tennis—I seldom win, but don't consider myself a loser—it's for fun/relaxation and exercise. HOW DID I GET INTO THIS? The after-dinner conversation is where I intended to go.

I'll aim toward connecting this "ending" log to the beginning—written about 14 weeks ago. Rereading it strikes me again, as it did when I recalled it, that the connections are myriad. "Form" occurs twice, as in "sleep paralysis . . . necessary for other forms to be activated." One is trans-formed in this stage of sleep to a physiological state somewhat like death. Perhaps this liberates the "mind" in ways we can not fathom . . . and allows THE ULTIMATE CONNECTION with the universe! I can't explain the almost telepathic symbolism of this remembered dream.

"I have taken something that doesn't belong to me." The knowledge of FUTURE readings—already present in mind? " . . . takes a very long time . . . wrong turns . . . discover the way back, to return it. "It's always been there, undiscovered, and returning it is ethical—not a moral or legal issue."

"It's very late . . . give up . . . I want so to return it before it is missed." Is it mine? Do I really have what "it" takes (and gives!)? I have "committed" no crime—if I "commit" to "return" what has been held "within."

"It is not clear . . . until context is available." " . . . 19th Century . . . I dart in and out of the institutions . . . " An apt metaphor for 16th & 17th Century conflicting world views? Then there's the context of *The Glass Bead Game* and his—(Hesse, 1969) Castalia, Kuhn, Bateson, and all the others—connections lend richness to the metaphor "in mind!" & "out there!" " . . . loaded with my unzipped shoulderbag, a portable TV, a cassette recorder, and a cloth drawstring bag . . . filled with oranges (?) and dull pointed objects sticking out of the bag, not coming through—but making it hard to maneuver." My "bag" remains unzipped—not closed . . . portable TV: symbolic of sight-vision (grainy and course), trans-portable and light (lite) . . . Recorder: "all the better to hear you with . . . " and to remember? And THEN: ROUND (oranges?) Objectives—dull, sticking out, but not coming THRU the drawstring bag! Connects to (pointless) theories built upon errors without a chance for breakthru—contained in context—making it harder and harder to "manuever." Or, are they "fresh" undiscovered, contained in an outmoded "cloth drawstring" context?

"Coming up behind . . . three threatening forms . . . one on my right is trying to control my path . . . pushing me toward the two on my left . . . (2 to 1 ratio? Atomic theory) drawing up a syringe . . . meant for meeeee!" One and one make three! Right—Left SPLITTING! Logic and/or Creativity? Both—And! What is contained in the syringe?

" . . . my bag is unzipped—my hands full. I made it this far alone . . . I NEED HELP! . . . no one is aware of my plight unless I open my mouth." My appeal is to "a higher power!" I haven't the "faintest," WHY it is Reagan? That's enough to jolt (any LIBERAL) back to consciousness!

Somehow I picture you reading this—with the by now familiar "Mona Lisa" smile you "wear" so well! The one I part-ialized during this co-evolutionary "leap" of a *class!*—with foresight, prolongation of reference, internalized, stratified, and reCONSTITUTED—was meant for me! I know it is for all the others—but when it comes my way it's " . . . worth 10,000 words . . . " received with respect and gratitude. (making me stretch . . .)

A final quote and request (last).

From "A Teacher's Connection," by Will Gillett, Assoc. prof. of Computer Science, Wash. U.:

"We know the University is here as a mainstay of knowledge—but that's just a bunch of esoteric stuff, just words. If you finally experience and understand the discovery of this knowledge—if you discover through your research knowledge never thought of in this world before—nothing big like Einstein's theory of relativity but *some small thing*—you want to *perpetuate it.* You've worked on a problem and you *finally see it*—this really neat thing that leads you to see this o*th*er thing and that o*th*er thing. Through the knowledge you've discovered, you're *connected with a broader world of knowledge."*

"If you really perceive knowledge to be important then you want to *give this gift to someone else.* If you're silly enough to get a Ph.D. and you've spent all this time *searching for knowledge,* then it's built into you, *I think, to want to give it back.* If you can teach, if you know how to get things across to others, it is personally satisfying to see the light dawn in someone's eyes. That's a big part of teaching . . . " (*Washington U. Magazine* Winter 1986). *Reflections on Teaching.*

Gillett said it so well—I wanted to share it with you—I think it reflects both (of us) And the paths we share. Finally, and I have been known to "jump the gun" before, when it comes 'round, to the time I have the privilege of choosing my dissertation advisor—I want YOU! As I wrote in my term paper—"the map is constructed as the distance is traveled" I feel certain that there can be no other who can "tap, expand—even sustain" the process, both—and, when liberated. In-formal as this is—when the time comes—context will prevail. It feels soo good to "stretch . . . "

I plan to "dive" again in the same place. I'm sure I'll find "other" dishes on the menu.—Great meals are hard to repeat.

[What you must look for is another meal, not better or worse, but different and equally as great. I'm glad you enjoyed! I look forward to tiptoeing through other menus in the future. D.S.B.]

Epi-log: 1988

Dorothy Stroh-Becvar, Ph.D., did consent to chair my dissertation advisory committee. She was chairperson as I began, February 1987, and was, as this reaction log shows, a strong directing influence for any graduate student willing to "stretch and develop" intellectual muscle; this log gives special re-cognition to her as "perturbing the system" to bring forth that which intuitively gifted teachers know is within grasp for students. However, in May 1987, the "Becvarian" systems team (Dorothy and Ray Becvar, Ph.D., its founding member) resigned their teaching positions at SLU, moving to positions with better "fit" for these dynamic creative masters of cybernetic systems.

J. J. O'Brien, Ph.D., consented to chair-position of my dissertation committee—"giving me my head," saying "now, do it your way—I'm with you all the way—it's your dissertation." Rick Bender, Ph.D., said, "I'll read it when it's done." John DiTiberio, Ph.D., joined the committee, forming a triad, stepping in as the solitary member and "new" head of the Department of Individual, Marriage & Family Development and Therapy as an admitted "newcomer" to cybernetics and systems theory, having come from psychology. "J. J.," beloved mentor, liberated me for the process of self-liberation. Rick eventuated the necessary scholarly mode, and John potentiated at least two "intellectual breakthroughs" by insisting "It's not yet clear . . . "

The first instance perturbed the natural involvement of a fuzzy pattern organizing my theorizing thought/thesis of higher levels of education change—the dissonance and meta double-binds experienced by graduate students at L. II, and the CYBERNETIC SHOCK of L. III (where lies cybernetic epistemology)—to Bateson's (1972) theoretical Learning Levels of Change (Zero thru IV). "Directed" back to base, I found this "fit" of theoretical concepts "snug," and so did John. These "systems checks" sessions were intellectually and emotionally agonizing for both John and me. He'd offer, I'd feel provoked. "It gets clearer each time," brought me back to earth and my responsible relentless efforts to make it clear. Several at-home phone calls from me notified John when I had "re-viewed" and was into major "re-vision" and was about to make an evolutionary all-systems-go launch, re-calibrating my (re-constituted) course, along paths emerging from our sessions. Intuitively I wanted to let him know our sessions were not in vain. Finally, as I was untangling myself from my own emotional underwear and my "me against thee" attitude, it came to mind that change of committee and multiple edits/differing perspectives had evolved the nearly total loss of the organizing conceptual PATTERN THAT CONNECTED my writing/thoughts!

The guiding light of *traditional, residual,* and *emergent framework*—was in my head—but not in my manuscript! I had "buried" it on the second page—never referring to it again, expecting John and any other uninitiated non-systems reader to "know" my path! More like a "re-entry moment" than a "turning point," replacing the words representing concepts, the pieces snapped in place forming the whole, like polar opposites attract, when turned the "right" way, the structural framework re-stored and re-constructed . . . the final re-vision was accepted. A year later, May 1988, I had written this dissertation/book, fulfilling the final requirement for Doctorate in Philosophy.

It was "J.J." who introduced me to "the 'it'/is the process leading to 'it' "—this book reflects the process of "Ph.D.-ing." The whole *is* greater than the sum of its parts. This is my way of "giving back that something I did not take," of my dream, that which was mentored by each of these professors in his/her own way—and is meant to be given again to someone else. Much of my dream, logged that first morning after I invented the "elephant in the road" and had tasted the first morsel, that Spring of '86, comes back now—particularly the symbols of the "three threatening gowned, hooded forms . . . one on my right trying to control my path and pushing me bodily toward the two on my left, one of whom is drawing up a syringe I'm afraid is meant for me! . . . I NEED HELP!" I suppose the "higher power" invocation of

Reagan makes sense to . . . as I wake up. Thinking about it now, the dream seems prophetic and metaphorically rich and boundless with connections . . . paradoxically, much of the future seems to lie in dreams re-called—or is it all "the dream of reality" that we "make come true"? Or, is it that we can't see "it" until we have the right metaphor to see "it"?

"The patterns that bind ideas together 'are as close as we can get to ultimate truth.' " [Bateson in Keeney, 1983, p. 46].

Beyond Revolutions . . .

CHAPTER 1
Introduction and Overview of World Views

Theme Statement and Definition of Terms

Cybernetic epistemology is the complex patterned steering knowledge involved in the "process of knowing, constructing and maintaining a world of experience" (Keeney, 1983, p. 108), the knowledge structuring one's experiential world. It is "a way of discovering and constructing alternative patterns in the ecology of our experience" (Keeney, 1983, p. 48.). Cybernetic processes broaden perspective—or re-structure world view. Bateson (1972) in *Steps to an Ecology of Mind* held: "Cybernetics is the biggest bite of the fruit of the Tree of Knowledge . . . taken in over 2000 years" (p. 476). Furthermore, Bateson (1972) equated a cybernetic epistemology with processes of "achieving Learning III change, [or] learning *about* learning" (p. 303).

References throughout literature are made to world view(s) and/or a call for a *change of world view*. World views were the dominant concern of the broad philosophical, historical, scientific, sociocultural recapitulations consulted in this study/inquiry. Yet the origins of world view commonly are treated as obvious knowledge, as if "every schoolboy knows . . . " (Bateson, 1979) without more than vague references as to whose and what world view is implied (pp. 23–64). Segal (1986) said: "our 17th century mentality manifests itself in daily life. . . . Most people see the world like 17th century scientists"; the applicability of 20th century relativity theory and quantum mechanics "has not touched the average person" (p.14). World views or philosophical orientations are unarticulated rules of the patterns organizing the world—and are seldom a topic of non-academic conversation. Furthermore, like politics and religion, views about them often compete and conflict. Popkewitz (1984) suggested the organizing conceptual frameworks used in this study of change of world view. It is patterned and organized as involving "traditional, residual, and emergent conceptual frameworks" (p. 187): (1) The world views of John Locke and Immanuel

Kant served as the traditional frame, (2) Kuhn's (1962, 1970) "Revolutions as Change of World View" (pp. 111–35) the residual, and (3) cybernetic epistemology as an emergent—and beyond conceptual frame.

The study used Rychlak's (1981) perspective on personality theory as its *traditional* frame. Rychlak (1981) distinguished the philosophical world views of Locke and Kant as the basis for personality theories. Elsewhere, Becvar (1986) listed their philosophical assumptions as "17th Century World Views" (Classnotes). Rychlak (1981) further attributed personality theories as structured and based on these opposing world views. Conceptually, he described 20th-century personality change dynamics as those of (1) Freudian internal "drives," (2) behaviorism's "needs" and "reinforcements," (3) humanism's/existentialism's "striving" toward "self-actualization and/or transcendence," to (4) present-day *change, cope and/or adjust,* dynamic patterns of the "so-called 'cognitive revolution' " (Efram and Lukens, 1986, p. 65).

In a *residual* frame, from the perspective of a conflict paradigm, Kuhn's (1962, 1970) metaphorical portrayal of "Revolutions as Changes of World View" introduced the conceptual pattern of paradigm shift. He wrote of a pattern of shift, from the historically dominant 17th-century world view of Locke's linear dichotomies and cause/effect thinking to a 20th-century world view of circular simple cybernetics (pp. 111–35). Kuhn's (1962, 1970) structural metaphor of *revolution* as change is punctuated as the residual frame meaning what has become, in the language of the marketplace, "settled as the bottom-line" (Segal, 1986, p. 15) out of conflicting traditional world views. Revolutions in thinking, or paradigm shift, progress through patterned process of competition and conflict, in what Kuhn (1970) defended as "not vicious" circles (p.176; p. 208). This circular pattern involved what Watzlawick, Beavin, and Jackson (1967) metaphorically called "Games Without End" (pp. 232–36). In the twenty-five years since Kuhn (1962) introduced paradigm theory, simple (circular) cybernetics has evolved, now addressing meta-cybernetic patterns of feedback, recursion, self-reference, paradox, autonomy, and now the "sacred" (Bateson and Bateson, 1987).

The study's *emergent* frame theorists held with a "new epistemology." They recognized the pattern of cognitive dissonant (Festinger, 1957) double-binds and the shock of cybernetics of Bateson's (1972) theory of Logical Learning levels of change, which is involved in changing world views. In a nuclear age, conflict paradigm or a pattern depicting *revolution* as the dynamic force for broad change has ramifications that are no longer resolutory. Emergent quantum physics, relativity theory, and late-20th-century technology have evolved the overriding issue of this age: the pattern of the organized, unrelenting march toward nuclear holocast. Twentieth-century world view has, out of necessity, gone "metacontextual" (Keeney, 1983, p. 43) to Kuhn's (1962, 1970) pattern of "competition and conflict," to involve ecological universal views. Non-hierarchical meta-contextual views overarch either/or thinking (out of which dissonance arises) and instead introduce "Cooperation, not competition as the sine qua non of social existence" (von Foerster, cited in Segal, 1986, p. 4). There are no winners in a nuclear war.

Dominant sociocultural and educational processes and praxes of the past trained students in the necessity of empirical truths, understanding, prediction, and control. Responsible higher education now re-educates them in cybernetic epistemology. In the process, it is hypothesized that students experience cognitive dissonance or discomfort and psychological tension (Festinger, 1957; Bateson's Learning II). For a time, a cybernetic epistemology (Bateson's Learning III) involved warranted but institutionally illicit confusion and concern or *cybernetic shock;* taken on, this new epistemology is seen by some as "becoming a non-conformist." Cybernetic shock manifests itself like Toffler's (1970) *Future Shock,* as students who have cut their teeth on the structure of traditional and residual world views encounter the complexity of heretofore "invisible" meta-cybernetic patterns of recursion, self-reference, paradox and autonomy. The duration and degree of cybernetic shock undoubtedly varies from student to student as they covertly ponder and generate questions taken as understood at Learning levels I and II. They conduct a meta-search for reduction or resolution of dissonance that they experience inherent in the dominant pattern of a shared conflict paradigm of traditional/residual world views. Broad questions evolve concerning the who, what, when, where, why, and *how* one becomes a cybernetic epistemologist. Paradoxically, Keeney (1983) stated that to become a cybernetic epistemologist is to "acknowledge that we always have been cybernetic epistemologists. The 'trick' is to be a cybernetic epistemologist and *know* it" (p. 69).

Purpose of the Inquiry

The review of the literature indicated the need to study some key patterns involved in historical, philosophical, scientific, cultural, and social bases for epistemological assumptions or how we know what we think we know. (If one is to change, finding out *what* one knows is essential.) In a residual frame, Kuhn (1962, 1970) theoretically held that it is in surveying the rich experimental literature . . . [which] makes one suspect that something like a paradigm is prerequisite to perception itself. What a man sees depends both upon what he looks at and also upon what his previous visual-conceptual experience has taught him to see.*

[p. 113]

Provocatively, historically dominant paradigms of the past comprise the thesis of Burke's (1986) *The Day the Universe Changed* in that "We are what we know. And when the body of knowledge changes, so do we" (p. 11). Bateson (1972) held that knowledge is "the difference that makes a difference." "Information" is knowledge meta or learning *about* learning (L. III) (p. 453).

Fundamentally, our "previous visual-conceptual experience has taught" (Kuhn, 1962, 1970, p. 113) that a shift to a cybernetic epistemology is experienced as a *revolution* in thinking—comparable to Kuhn's description of paradigm shifts in the scientific community. Paradigm shift bears likeness to what Ferguson (1980) called "Pendulum swing" (pp. 71–3). Nevertheless, Kuhn's (1962, 1970) persistent metaphor of revolution or shift is described as cybernetic. He defended this "intrinsically circular" pattern in his 1970 limited revision: "Postscript-1969" cited that "not all circularities are vicious" (p. 176, p. 208).

The purpose of this study is to describe heuristically the patterned process and praxis of interaction (cognitive dissonance and cybernetic shock) as experienced by graduate students, using "new epistemological tricks" that Keeney (1983) held we have always had (p. 60). It is a beginning attempt to illuminate the theme of world view change. As Bateson and Bateson (1987) suggested in *Angel's Fear* [to tread]: "Towards an Epistemology of the Sacred," the experience of "learning to learn *about* contexts of contexts (L.III)" or change of world view may account in part for the complex nature of cognition. It attempts illumination of how epistemological patterns of higher level learning change evolve, according to Bateson's (1972) Logical Learning Levels Zero through IV (pp. 280–308).

Inquiry Statement

The Individual, Marriage and Family Development and Therapy major area at St. Louis University is a graduate level program in

**The Structure of Scientific Revolutions* (Chicago: University of Chicago Press, 1962, 1970) © 1962.

education & counseling, a program of inquiry directed toward the search for knowledge and understanding as potential for disclosing the structure of truth. This can be a disconcerting process, for as John Dewey remarked in *Experience and Nature:*

> Surrender of what is possessed, disowning of what supports one in secure ease, is involved in all inquiry and discovery; the latter implicate an individual still to make, with all the risks implied therein. For to arrive at new truth and vision is to alter (p. 245).

The marriage and family major at St. Louis University has been philosophically committed to the tenents of systems theory, which favors what has been termed cybernetic epistemology. Cybernetic epistemology or "steering knowledge" differs from more traditional epistemologies or world views in that one focuses on broad, complex organizational patterns of recursive feedback in interactional sequences rather than on singular linear cause/effect, either/or demonstrative thinking. "Understanding cybernetic epistemology may completely alter one's habits of actions . . . epistemology is the deepest order of change" (Keeney, 1983, p. 6); profound change is re-cognized at higher learning levels. In this study of the experience of patterns involving epistemological change the heuristic mode of inquiry is used. Heuristic Inquiry is a mode of research in which "formal hypotheses play no part"; instead it attempts "to uncover and disclose that which is as it is." This type of study/inquiry is meant to illuminate a theme and to formulate questions to further understanding and knowledge of change (Douglass and Moustakas, 1985, p. 42). It seems probable that a student's introduction to and involvement in the concepts and patterned operational process of at least that aspect of systems theory labeled cybernetic epistemology may provoke intellectual and emotional responses that could often be described as patterned dissonance and *cybernetic shock*. This study/inquiry is an attempt to find out if that is the case. This sort of study is important because it will provide some check on whether, for the students involved, their education is organized, as Jane Rowland Martin expressed it, as a journey of alienation or integration. In particular, as Gowin (1972, Thomas, Ed.) described: "Studies in logic or epistemology . . . may be valid in themselves, but, unless a special study is made bringing findings over into the educational context, nothing follows for educational practice" (p. 15).

Theoretical Assumptions—Broadening Perspective

Chapter 2 provides a review of the literature and the philosophical, historical, scientific, cultural, and social background of this study/inquiry. It is fundamental to a cybernetic epistemology, according to G. Spencer Brown's Laws of Form (Keeney, 1983) "to begin by drawing a distiction" and, further, to punctuate in order to narrow the breadth of the "problem" (p. 18). (Conceptual punctuation draws attention to a higher order of recursive feedback process than the drawing of distinction; see glossary for terms.) Consistent with these laws of form, the conceptual framework for this study is both philosophical and historical; as Popkewitz (1981) suggested, it is arranged in "traditional, residual [conflict views], and emergent [cooperative view] conceptual frames" (p. 187).

A description of the philosophical *traditional* 17th-century frame for this study is provided. Even though historically a century separates their lives, Rychlak (1981) described Locke's and Kant's views of the world as competitive and conflicting, mixed or integrated. In this spirit their assumptions span centuries in the way they pit phenomena opposite one another as versus each other or as verses. As has been touched upon earlier, Rychlak (1981) defined perspectives on personality as either/or or mixed; "internal conflict" is the patterned motivational dynamic in the dominant world view (p. 31). In this study, assumptions framed as coming out of the 17th century (Becvar, 1986) are considered as they span subsequent eras even into the 20th century.

Next this study employs Kuhn's (1962, 1970) punctuation of scientific revolution as a pattern of simple circular "cybernetic" process. For this study such a metaphor provides a *residual* frame, reflecting a persistent conflict paradigm, for the way we were for a very long time before knowing cybernetic epistemology. That is, as Keeney (1983) claimed, "a 'systems,' 'non-lineal,' 'ecological,' or '*circular*' epistemology may or may not signify a cybernetic epistemology (p. 95) . . . The image of a circle is not the best way to think of recursion" (p. 59). The pattern of organization of revolution is circular, thereby neglects recursion.

The new epistemology explores meta-recursive patterns *emergent and beyond* either/or double-binds of contemporary conceptualizations of "problem solving" psychology and of " 'self'-concepts" (ie., self-worth/self-esteem) at Bateson's Learning Level II. Bateson (1972) claimed that re-structured learning *to* learn (L. II) "is to become flexible as the categories of eternal 'contraries' burst open with Learning III" change or learning *about* learning (p. 305). Part of the "trick" is in "changing our conceptual lens from material to [recursive] pattern, rather than parts to wholes" (p. 95). It may well be that the cultural/habitual punctuation of Kuhn's (1962, 1970) circular pattern of *revolutions* has become the most dominant motivational dynamic for change. Bateson held there are "patterns that connect" all of *Mind and Nature* (Bateson, 1979; Keeney, 1983, p. 97.) and that "the organization of living things depends on circular and more complex chains of determination" (Bateson, 1979, p. 203). *Revolutionary* metaphors hold that we must fight first and then shift. Similarly, the constructivist philosopher Heinz von Foerster (1949) draws the distinction of a (Lockean) mechanistic world view as involving patterns of "circular casual feedback mechanisms" with emphasis on material power rather than pattern. He called this a "partial (objective) view" (cited in Segal, 1986, p. xv); that is, material reality comprises only part of one's view. Conceptually, this "Radical constructivism" has taken on the "unpopular job of shattering the fantasy of objective reality" (p. 3) of revolutionary structured patterns.

The difficulties of change of world view, according to von Foerster and Marturana in Segal's (1986) *The Dream of Reality,* involves structured linguistic patterns. Pertinent is the

> relationship between language, thinking and our view of reality. Language, operating below our level of every day consciousness, structures our thinking by punctuating circular streams of interaction into one-way causalities. It nominalizes processes and unwittingly seduces us into habitual causal schemes for explaining the world.
>
> [p. 58–59]

As so, Kniskern (1983) claimed that it is in neglecting the outside organizational or meta "larger patterns" that leads scientists to a "distorted view of the world" (p. 38). He agreed with Keeney (1983), who stated that "the drawing of 'partial arcs' and the mapping of the world into parts provides us with various pragmatic advantages. The danger of using the punctuations of partial arcs is that they are approximations of the whole patterns of recursion" (cited in Kniskern, 1983, p. 60).

Then, again, as Bateson (1979) held, "the organization of living things depends upon circular and more complex chains of determination" (p. 103) and that these are characterized by "many negative loops" or double-binds (p. 199). Patterns of recursion have to do with negative feedback processes in the organization of broad interactional sequences. This mystifying pattern of organizational process is the "Strange Loopiness" involved in what Nobel laureate Hofstadter (1979) called *The Eternal Golden Braid:* two strands found looping recursively entwined in a three-stranded pattern connecting all living matter; it is described as structured much like the DNA molecule.

This study thus views Kuhn's (1962, 1970) circular model as representative of a recursive negative feedback process suggestive of what he called "Invisible Revolutions" (pp. 136–43); that is, linear and simple circular "mis-constructions" render meta-organized patterns of revolution "invisible" (p. 140); the recursive patterns of conflict at a meta-level of cybernetics are concealed by a circular description. Accordingly, Kuhn's Revolution Model (Becvar, 1986) is described, defined, and illustrated. This circular structure also enfolds a conceptual model of cybernetics that describes and explains orders of recursion—as the meta-picture surfaces. In addition, as Bateson (1979) suggested, "Binocular Vision" (pp. 69–70) is employed to suggest and sharpen the image of cybernetic complementarity at a recursive, so-called synthesizing meta-level. In this case, patterns organizing "Corrective Vision for A Binocular View" (Fraser, 1984) "may not be enriching but enraging when we attempt to move usefully through our world" (pp. 43–57). Patterned illustrations are also presented.

Emergent theorist Keeney's (1983) aesthetic frame is used to describe and to connect the similar pattern of traditional epistemology of the 17th century to the residual view of Kuhn's Revolution Model (Becvar, 1986) consistent with the cybernetic assumption of recursion as "reciprocity." Keeney (1983) held that conflicting views differ yet relate holistically and through recursion connect rather than split nature. Varela (cited in Keeney, 1983) formulated and invoked "double discription" (pp. 37–44) to describe patterns, organization, and relationships. Emergent frame cybernetic epistemology, recursion, or reciprocity, as constructed by Varela, is defined as: "the it"/"the process leading to it" (p. 92), which yields another patterned illustrated model. Varela's formula is applied to both the dichotomy of Locke versus Kant and Kuhn's Revolution Model (Becvar, 1986), rendering an autonomous account and patterned illustration of the "larger cybernetic of cybernetics picture." A contextual inclusive binocular view has ushered entry into the emergent—and beyond "dangerous" Learning III territory (Bateson, 1972, p. 305).

At the convergence of historical traditional, residual, emergent—and beyond categorical frames, a process pattern of "transient therapeutic triangulation" and "Equilateral Geodetic triangulation" is illustrated and defined. These two patterned illustrations serve as preface to description and consideration of Jantsch's (1980) eminently complex paradigm of co-evolution. His complex theory of "Universal self-organization" gave example to a cybernetic syntheses of new emergent and beyond concepts. Also considered is von Foerster's (1973) constructivism, which is "structure coupled" with Maturana's (1975, 1978) theory of structure determinism (cited in Segal, 1986). A pattern of cooperative nurturance emerges between theorists. These emergent theorists' constructs reflect an allegiance to what Douglas (1976) referred to as the "Classical-cooperative paradigm" (pp. 39–54) or what according to Capra (1983) qualifies them as "Bootstrapper's: " being "able to view any number of different partially successful models without favoritism," recognizing that theoretically "patterns do not 'contain' one another but rather 'involve' one another" (pp. 94) with a change of process of learning at Learning Level III. A "Bootstrapper's" approach is one that

> abandons the idea of fundamental building block of matter . . . accepts no fundamental entities . . . constants, laws, or equations. The universe is seen as a *dynamic web* of interrelated events. None of the properties of any part of the web is fundamental; they all follow from the properties of the other parts and the overall consistency of their interrelations determines the structure of the entire web. [Chew, cited in Capra, 1983, p. 93.]
>
> [see figure 7, p. 57] . . .

Emergent and beyond views are those theories that seem to co-evolve using the bootstrapper's approach in harmony with a cooperative paradigm. According to Briggs and Peat (1984), "what Kuhn termed a paradigm shift . . . means putting aside our assumptions on how the world works. This is an uncomfortable thing to do" (p. 230), involving patterns of organized dissonant double-binds at Learning Level II. A cybernetic epistemology is defined and is synonymous with a change of one's processes of learning. It involves *cybernetic shock* of the complexity of infinite patterns of L. III. Similarly, it means putting aside our assumptions of how *to* learn (L. II)—and learning to learn *about* learning (L. III). The change to learning *about* learning is also an uncomfortable thing to do—involving patterns of confusion and concern or *cybernetic shock*.

Importance of the Study/Inquiry

Again, according to Burke (1986, p. 11), "when the body of knowledge changes, so do we." However, Kuhn (1962, 1970) asked, "How do scientists proceed when aware only that something has gone fundamentally wrong at a [Learning III] *level* with which their training has not equipped them to deal?" (p. 86.) Graduate students involved in the phenomenon of paradigm shift (similar to this study/inquiry) in the context of a residual frame of revolution fit Kuhn's (1962, 1970) description of early sixties gestalt experiments on doctoral students as research subjects fitted with inverted lens goggles:

> At the start his perceptual apparatus functions as it had been trained to function . . . the result is extreme disorientation, and acute personal crisis. But after the subject has begun to deal with his new world, his entire visual field flips over, usually after an intervening period in which vision is simply confused. The assimilation of a previously anomalous field has reacted upon and changed the field itself. Literally as well as metaphorically, the man . . . has undergone a revolutionary transformation of vision.* [p. 112]

In the eighties, reversal of visual images also interested Briggs and Peat (1984), who commented on Kuhn's work in *Looking Glass Universe*. Their view follows:

> Even people who admire . . . Kuhn may not realize how bizarre his revelations really are. . . . [His] analysis implies that science has always been a looking glass enterprise in a looking glass universe—we just didn't notice . . . [invisible recursion]. Attitudes [of revolution] might seem as well-worn and inevitable as our skin. So leaving them behind might generate some discomfort.
>
> [p. 18]

The importance of this study is related to broad socio-cultural (political, economic, ecological, et al.) exclusive use of traditional and residual frame images or metaphors based on a conflict paradigm that seems to involve humanity in a patterned symmetrical escalating "Game Without End," which paradoxically may end in "catastrophe" (Watzlawick, Weakland, and Fisch, 1974, p. 22). Patterns of competition and conflict are, according Keeney (1983): "The major epistemological issues . . . concerned with the consequences of particular habits of punctuation" (p. 96), like that of the metaphorical/actual dominant punctuation of *revolution* as the motivational dynamic for change. Catherine Bateson (1985) punctuated physical metaphors that, in a nuclear age, "do not transfer . . . [are] no longer appropriate, no longer able to carry the burden that would make it [revolution] a basis for ethical decision" (p. 44). For this study Kuhn's Revolution Model (Becvar, 1986) serves as a punctuated residual point for re-constructing alternative patterns that in the past facilitated "progress and growth"

**The Structure of Scientific Revolutions* (Chicago: University of Chicago Press, 1962, 1970), © 1962.

based on "competition and conflict" or the "natural and necessary" pattern of organization of "Revolutions as Change of World View" (Kuhn, 1962, 1970, pp. 111–35). A cybernetic epistemology and the punctuated emergent universal views of this study reflect a re-constituted pattern of cooperation and ethical tolerance harmonious with "becoming: " a Learning Level III change (Bateson, 1972, p. 301). Ecologically, von Foerster's construct is that "Life is a non-zero sum game: all players win or all players lose. Cooperation, not competition is the sine qua non of social existence. The price of this world view . . . [is] to replace the notion of objectivity with that of responsibility" (cited in Segal, 1986, p. 4) toward humanity and the environment.

Hypothesized cognitive dissonance (Festinger, 1957) is a function of the perceived lack of pattern fit between emergent and traditional and/or residual frames. The study/inquiry of the shock of complex cybernetic contextual recursion, which coincides with learning *about* learning (Learning III), may be a very preliminary act, a partial answer to the question of pattern of organization Keeney (1983) asked: "What is the structure of our experiential world?" (p. 107.) The aim of this study, like that of constructivists, "is not to find fault with traditional epistemologies, but to account [in part] for cognition, the totality of our mental faculties" (Segal, 1983, p. 4). Cognitive processes involving epistemology explore *how* one structures or constructs views of the world (inside-out). Perspective reflects one's point of view or what structures one perceives as Reality (outside-in).

Heuristic Approach

A review of the literature of key meta-perspectives provides a historical, philosophical, scientific, and sociocultural base for this investigative study. The investigator is a participant observer in the major area of Individual, Marriage and Family Development and Therapy, of the Department of Counseling Education at St. Louis University. To the researcher, graduate students in the process of learning *about* learning seemed to manifest patterns of cognitive dissonance (Festinger, 1957) in synchrony with "paradigm shift." Becoming a cybernetic epistemologist involves learning *about* a change of world view. Students experienced it like another *revolution* (Kuhn, 1962, 1970, pp. 111–35). *Cybernetic shock* for the sample interviewed seemed manifest and consistent with becoming a cybernetic epistemologist, a process of learning change meta to learning *to* learn (L. II)—or learning *about* learning (L. III). As an investigative study of the experience of change of world view involving patterns of dissonant double-binds and the shock of cybernetic complexity, this study employed the "un-methodology" that Douglass and Moustakas (1985) represented as "Heuristic Inquiry: The Internal Search to Know" (pp. 39–55). Generally, heuristic inquiry as a framework "offers a disciplined pursuit of essential meanings connected with everyday human experience" (p.39). Its emphasis is on patterns of organizing "reflective learning—that reflection is a process of creating and clarifying the meaning of experience in terms of self in relation to self and self in relation to others" (p. 40). The approach offered a research model appropriate for a meta-search for patterns of "discovery of meaning and essence in significant human experience" via process patterns of "reflecting, exploring, sifting, and elucidating the nature of the phenomenon under investigation" (p. 40).

Moreover, this "fresh approach" (Douglass and Moustakas, 1985, p. 39) is "consistent with the tone of the *1972 NSSE Yearbook,* edited by Thomas, (1972), [which] argues the need for new research paradigms." Indeed, Shulman (1970, 1981) pictured "a research community with equally valid, alternative methods for asking different kinds of questions, where the value of quantitative and qualitative approach are on par" (cited in Allender, 1986, pp. 173–93).

Research "Un-methodology"

Following the heuristic mode, an effort was made to illuminate patterns of organization/structure of graduate student intellectual and emotional responses to the program of studies. Graduate student responses involved that they were expected to understand, "know" or "become" cybernetic epistemologists as part of the change processes of study/learning. A representative sample of students at or beyond the study of Advanced Individual, Marriage and Family Therapy (ED 145–665) was interviewed to determine patterns of (1) altered intellectual and emotional response to their learning experience of cybernetic epistemology, (2) their perceptions of the duration and degree of these patterns of responses, and (3) an examination of what difference between students who did and those who did not acknowledge having experienced these patterned responses. Prior approval for all intrusive measures had been granted from the Institutional Review Board (IRB Protocol #4800,—June 18, 1987). No attempt was made to offer primary definitions of intellectual or emotional direction. What was of concern was what labels students felt could be applied to their responses. No effort was made to offer precise quantification of the duration and degree to which these responses prevailed. (In some cases they were asked for a subjective rating, on a scale of 1 to 10, from low to high, of experienced depth/intensity of dissonance/shock.) The findings were not generalizable beyond the population surveyed. Literature on those aforementioned key historical/philosophical patterns of epistemological thought (e.g., linear, circular, recursive, et cetera), since the 17th century served to guide the design of interview questions and an interpretation of the results. Special attention was given to aspects of cybernetic epistemology that deal with *why* and *how* the persistent dominant motivational dynamic or *revolutions* is involved with change of world view.

Limitations of the Study/Inquiry

The parameters set provide a description of the pattern of experience involved in becoming a cybernetic epistemologist, an attempt at Learning III in the area of higher education mentioned. The study further attempts illumination and interpretation of views in light of the (1) traditional 17th-century world views, (2) the residual view of Kuhn's Model of Revolution (Becvar, 1986), (3) a cybernetic epistemology, and emergent universal views. The literature review employed a pattern of traditional/residual comparative analysis combined with an emergent heuristic cybernetic form and pattern synthesis, consistent with the processes of becoming a cybernetic epistemologist. As Babbie (1983) indicated, this method generally has "more validity but less reliability," than empirical quanitiative methods, and "results cannot be generalized as safely" (p. 270). The replication of its patterns would pose difficulties, and "conclusions are seen as tentative rather than definitive" (Wagenaar and Babbie, 1983, p. 140).

On the other hand, the emergent heuristic approach to human scientific research does offer a "disciplined pursuit of essential meaning connected with everyday" and significant human experience. Through dialogue in audio-taped interviews focused on "inherent [patterns of] processes and values, we hope to develop a fresh perspective for the understanding of and application to scientific investigation" (Douglass and Moustakas, 1985, p. 39).

Summary

This introductory chapter has given an overview of the theme and a preliminary definition of some key terms (a protracted glossary follows the final chapter), along with statements about the purpose, inquiry, importance, heuristic approach and un-methodology, and limitations of this study and inquiry. The theoretical assumptions of chapter 2 are outlined, framed, and patterned as involving "traditional, residual and emergent" concepts (Popkewitz, 1984, p. 187).

Chapter 2 presents the body of the literature review. First, the review examines the patterned network of assumptions of Rychlak (1981), using Becvar's (1986) punctuation of the 17th-century world views of Locke and Kant as the historical *traditional* bases for world views. Next, Kuhn's Model of Revolutions (Becvar, 1986) provides a *residual* frame, followed by a preview of cybernetics. Also presented is a "binocular view" whose goal was a meta-level synthesis consistent with one "trick" of becoming a cybernetic epistemologist. Further process tricks are revealed by Varela (cited in Keeney, 1983) and Bateson's (1972, 1979, 1987) Logical Learning Level changes—Zero to IV. Finally, the *emergent/beyond* views of Jantsch's (1980) ultra-complex patterns of his co-evolutionary paradigm of a self-organizing universe, von Foerster's (1973) constructivism, Maturana's (1975, 1978) theory of structure determinism, and a view of Broderick's (1983) theoretical "transient therapeutic triangulation" evolve are described and patterns illustrated. (A review of the literature precedes each of the two remaining chapters in the attempt to convey the broad patterns of organization implicated as involved in change of world view.)

Chapter 3 presents, in its introductory remarks, the research approach dilemma according to further review of the literature. The heuristic approach and the un-methods of heuristic inquiry that embody research processes of immersion, acquisition, and realization are described. The method of realization involved intentionality, verification in intersubjectivity, and dissemination of the data as this dissertation. The research synthesis came from logged transcriptions of focused audio-taped interviews/dialogue with a sample of (N = 7) graduate student respondents.

The final chapter (4) synthesizes "student factors and cybernetic shock" first according to the related literature. The pattern of the process of heuristic realization continues then, in a reflective mode, with a participant-observer experiential account of cybernetic shock—involved in becoming a cybernetic epistemologist—in the attempt to illuminate further the theme of change of world view and the questions it generated. Realization of heuristic learning *about* learning or L.III involved verification and dissemination of the concepts of "student factors and cybernetic shock." Final realization is from the synthesis of the expressed verbal content (EVC) of transcribed interview tapes. The interviews focused on categories, themes, and patterns of intellectual and emotional responses to dissonance and shock involved in higher level learning, the process of becoming a cybernetic epistemologist—or change of world view. Douglass and Moustakas (1985) held: "It is here that a whole is assembled from the fragments and disparate elements that have been generated during the search" (p. 52). Bateson (1979) described the patterns of tacit and emergent concerns of this study/inquiry in an unfolding conversation with his daughter:

> **Father:** Any species can get into an evolutionary cul-de-sac . . . and be a party to its own extinction. . . . The world of mental process, is both tautological and ecological . . . a slowly self-healing tautology. . . . So, the tautology is broken; it's only pushed up to the next level of abstraction, the next logical level. That's so.
>
> **Daughter:** But how many levels are there?
>
> **Father:** No [sic], that I cannot know . . . whether it is ultimately a tautology nor how many logical levels it has. I am inside it and therefore cannot know its outer limits—if it has any.
>
> [pp. 206—208]

Chapter 2 begins the literature review with the categorical distinction of the *traditional* frame. The study punctuates, in patterns of description and illustrations, the assumptions of Locke and Kant (Rychlak, 1981) as versus world views originating in the 17th century yet infiltrating the *residual* mid–twentieth century frame of Kuhn's (1962, 1970) model of *revolutions* as change of world view.

CHAPTER 2
Review of the Literature of World Views

17th Century to Revolutions to Cybernetics . . . and Beyond

According to Segal (1986), the patterns of organization and structure of "Our 17th century mentality manifests itself in daily life . . . most people see the world like 17th century scientists" mechanistic (Lockean) and based on objective "Truth, Understanding and Reality. . . . Although relativity theory and quantum mechanics have radically altered the physicist's view of reality, this shift has not touched the average person" (p. 14). Philosophical orientations and unarticulated rules are seldom a topic of non-academic conversation. Like politics and religion, views about them often follow patterns of competition and conflict.

In Kuhn's (1962, 1970) portrayal of *The Structure of Scientific Revolutions,* he referred specifically to the pattern of paradigm shift from the historically dominant 17th century world view of linear dichotomies and cause/effect thinking to a 20th century world view of circular cybernetics. Therefore, this mid–20th century pattern of paradigm shift has its residual roots in the 17th-century mechanistic world view of Locke.

This study draws on Rychlak's (1981) century-spanning representation of the philosophical world views of John Locke and Immanuel Kant, using them as the historical traditional frame for studying patterns of personality and/or epistemology. The network of assumptions Rychlak (1981) described seem to fit Kuhn's (1970) patterned "constellation of received beliefs" (p. 175). It also follows the patterned "interpretive systems" of Becvar and Becvar (1982, pp. 27–31), the "belief system" of Ellis (1975, p. 119), as well as a pattern of organization and definition of a basic epistemology and/or personality.

The following pages first define and explain the assumption defined by Rychlak (1981) as Lockean and Kantian "because the differences in outlook they suggest are probably more familiar than any other set of terms. . . . The truth is that there has always been a division of this sort in the history of thought" (p. 16). According to Becvar and Becvar (1982), "a set of constructs of paired opposites" provide one's "interpretive frame" (p. 28).

Lockean Model

The world view of Locke stresses the prevalence of dualistic either/or thinking in its assumptions. Demonstrative reasoning is the overriding assumption in unipolarity (singularity) in meaning. Locke believed that the intellect is tabula rasa, or a blank slate, at birth and that all learning comes from the environment. His model of mentation moves from the simple to complex and is consistent with behaviorism. That is, he accepted constitutive mentality, mediation, and empirical determination of all that the mind represents. Small atomic units make up larger totalities, and patterns observed can always be reduced to smaller and smaller units for analysis.

Demonstrative reasoning involves the traits of singularity, linearity, unidirectionality, and non-contradiction. Processes focus on "primary and true" premises, closed to questions or alternatives (both Locke and Kant).

Objective view involves unipolar demonstrative meaning: reality and truth exist outside experience and intuition. The objective view assumes separation of the observer and the observed (Locke).

Linear reductionism involves the assumption that understanding anything can be broken down to final cause and effect (Locke).

Tabula rasa involves Locke's view of the mind as a "blank sheet." Environment "writes" on the blank slate *what* one then knows.

External reality involves the view of reality as separate from the observer; the "view" stimulates the senses. Perception is "outside-in" (Locke).

Realist view involves the content of minds as existing independent of mind "out there." Structured reality exists independent of the observer (Locke).

Theory of extraspective perspective frames things and/or events in the third person—the observer. "That, it" rather than "I, me" (objective, Lockean).

Empirical determinism involves knowledge as based solely on what can be observed. Consistent with a realist's perspective, truth is viewed as quantifiable (Locke).

Quantitative assumption involves a view of rigorous validation of objective criteria, describing the relationship between variables, empirical validation of predictions to support or disprove accepted theory (Locke).

Mediation view involves a theory of behaviorism. All things attributed to a self or identity are said to occur either/or, between incoming stimuli and outgoing results in patterned feedback loops. (Locke).

Pessimism involves a view that hope is unreasonable and that happiness, if attainable, lies beyond the sphere of ordinary experience. Locke's Model involves determinism in the form of final-cause/effect assumptions (mechanistic-deterministic; behavioristic).

Value-free judgment involves an instrumental theory of value, in that valuation should be based singularly on pleasures that result when acts are carried out. Acts leading to pleasure are good; those that lead to pain are bad (behavioristic assumptions; "is" dictates "ought"—Lockean).

Either/or thinking involves the historically dominant 17th century world view of linear *dichotomies* and final-cause and effect demonstrative reasoning of Locke (paradoxical meta–double-bind, see pp. 22–23).

Kantian Model

The overriding assumption of Kant generally involves both/and thinking. His philosophical view of human behavior stresses dialectical as well as demonstrative reasoning. He viewed intellect as pro forma. That is, categories of form, *patterns,* and cybernetic relationships exist a priori, before birth. Kant viewed noumenal *verses* (vss.) phenomenal experience as lending itself to meaningful understanding, transcendence, and prediction, as premises individually affirmed, rather than by the behaviorist form view of mediation.

Kantian philosophy used logic addressing orders (logos), which mind brings to bear as meaning. Finally, Kant's conceptualization philosophy is seen as an actively formative process according to which the individual shapes circumstances and categories; *patterns, shapes,* and *orders* are the ultimate source of understanding meaning.

Dialectical reasoning involves patterned traits of oppositionality, duality, relationality, contradiction, and arbitrariness. Processes focus on "synthesis" of "thesis and antithesis." (Kant is also demonstrative—both/and reasoning.)

Subjective view involves patterned constructed meanings that are private, difficult, or impossible to circumscribe, i.e., experiential, intuitive, self-referential, and paradoxical. The subjective view assumes the observer in that which is observed (Kant).

Cybernetic assumption is the complexity involving the general science of "steering" *patterns* and organization. The study of how processes of change determine various orders of stability and/or control; complex orders of recursion or feedback determine logical levels of stability and control or "change" (Kant).

Pro forma intellect involves the "a priori" assumption of patterned categories that act in a pro forma sense. Kantian philosophy presumes categories "exist" in the mind before birth—for the sake of form, patterns bring meaningful relations to the mind.

Perceptual constructed reality involves the view that reality is constructed as in the pattern individuals "observe;" through the pattern of senses reality comes to view; perception is "inside-out" (Kant).

Idealists or critical realists holds the view that the mind's contents, *what* we know, is in experience and intuition. Experiences are created by patterns in the mind.

Critical realists accept an experience called reality, but recognize personal or phenomenal parts of the pattern as the experience of reality (Kant). Critical skills develop a transfer effect on dissonance by addressing the dilemma of "fact vs. opinion"; intellect over emotions, e.g., $\frac{\text{intellect}}{\text{emotion}}$

Theory of introspective perspective frames events in the first person, from the autonomous perspective of an identity acting within, "I, me" rather than of "that, it" (subjective, Kant).

Noumenal vss. [*sic*] *phenomenal* involves Kant's philosophical view that we never know the noumenal world (one accepts that "things in themselves" exist), but we *order* it at the phenomenal level. Consistent with both/and thinking or "verses" views, Kant also held that the individual, through experience and unique sensory equipment, *orders* experiences into meaning—not merely as a response to stimuli. Thus ultimate truth is inaccessible, "truth" is "a multiverse—where many verses co-exist."

Qualitative assumptions involve a view of a patterned phenomenal realm, a cognitive or conceptual model; something is true if it makes immediate sense or patterned constructs have "face validity" (Kant).

Transcendence involves Kant's philosophy of the individual rising above customary understanding of experiences—even thinking in patterned opposition, questioning, analyzing, and reinterpreting those experiences—self-reflexively turning back on themselves to know what it is they know—critical thinking.

Optimism represents general hopefulness regarding the pattern of balance of pleasure and pain; Kant's Model is metaphysical and phenomenological in its account of the individual's role in the patterns of universal organization (organismic-living, humanistic).

Value-laden judgment involves an intrinsic theory of value, holding the worth of a thing or act can be due to its intrinsic merit. Duty and obligation are above dualistic pleasure and pain for positive value preferences (humanistic assumptions; "ought" dictates "is"—Kantian).

Both/and thinking involves a Kantian world view of cybernetic complexity of the patterns of organization.

As so Rychlak's (1981) definitions and explanation of the network of theoretical assumptions of Locke and Kant provocatively describe patterns of organization and reveal the structure of personality theory's basic conflict paradigm and its grasp on epistemology. Comparison and contrast comprehensively and penetratingly expose roots of a pattern of conflict and dissonance that goes back at least to 17th century world views.

Accordingly, Rychlak (1981) punctuated personality structure and its theories as patterned and based on one or the other world view or as mixed Kantian and Lockean. That is, psychoanalytic theory represents mixed world views in that it is constructed on mind versus body dualism, thereby accepting ordered patterns of *competing or conflicting* internal drives as its basic dynamic. Behaviorism is similarly constructed. However, it is theoretically categorized as Lockean, and to the competing/conflicting *drive* dynamics of psychoanalytic theoretical orientation it introduces patterns of *needs,* external/internal *motivation,* and *reinforcements.*

Phenomenological or humanistic/existential theories are constructed uniting the outlook of mind-body dualism and subjectivity. Their dynamic patterns emphasize *striving/transcendence* and *self-actualization* processes. Contemporary cognitive dynamics go beyond the patterned orders of conflict paradigm, to emphasize individual's as responsible for "*coping, adjusting,* or *changing*" their view of the world.

Rychlak (1981) summarized "the Kantian-versus-Lockean models and demonstrative-versus-dialectical meanings as . . . meta-theoretical assumptions . . . [as century-spanning] abstract universals because their meanings enter into so many understandings" (p. 821). This reflects the pattern of organization of personality theory's conflict paradigm view of the world (Douglas, 1976, pp. 55–83).

Becvar (1986) divided the theoretical assumptions defined and explained previously into Kantian and Lockean philosophical world views (figure 1, below). Accordingly, they fit Kuhn's (1962, 1970) description of exemplars or paradigm constellation gestalt "networks" (p. 175), the patterned "interpretive system" of Becvar and Becvar (1982, pp. 27–31), and the "belief system" of Ellis (1975, p. 119). This investigation employs this dualistic pattern of century-spanning assumptions in order to compare and contrast world views and understand the traditional patterns of process and praxis of organizing change of world view.

Figure 1. Seventeenth-century World Views of Locke and Kant*

LOCKEAN MODEL VERSUS KANTIAN MODEL

Demonstrative	Dialectical and Demonstrative
Objective	Subjective and Objective
Linear reductionism	Cybernetic complexity
Tabula rasa	Pro forma (a priori)
External reality	Perceptual constructed reality
Realist	Idealist-critical realist
Extraspective	Introspective
Empirical determinism	Noumenal vss. phenomenal
Truth as quantifiable	Ultimate truth inaccessible
Quantitative	Qualitative
Mediation	Transcendence
Pessimistic	Optimistic
Value-free	Value-laden
EITHER/OR THINKING	Both-and thinking
(Aristotle)	(Plato)
(Descartes)	(Einstein)
(Newton)	

*Becvar, Class Notes, 1986.

Thus the author defines in patterns of organization a contemporary *revolutionary* battlefield of competing and conflicting world views, consistent with "versus" views (figure 1, above). Yet a studied glance at the pattern of opposition yields a gigantic philosophical, paradoxical "meta—double-bind" (Weeks & L'Abate (1982), Locke's overriding assumption,

> "the *either/or* view of reality is a trap which denies us the ability to move to different frames of reference, to multiple alternatives . . . a problem can occur when one believes the solution to a difficulty is the implementation of that difficulty's opposite polarity" (italics added).
>
> [p. 90].

That is, a pattern of organization of shift to the opposite pole carries the paradoxical "illusion of choice" (Auger, 1987, pp. 49–53) with demonstrative either/or thinking. The *choice* of a single meta-perspective paradoxically binds the choice; one is stuck by the overriding either/or assumption to the meta-perspective involved—by this pattern of paradoxical meta–double-bind Weeks and L'Abate describe (1982, p. 43). In the following sections, as is described and illustrated, a pattern of shift, to the opposite pole, or an escalation of same pole activity pattern represents **no change.**

Residual Conceptual Framework—Kuhn's Revolution Model

It was theorized by Kuhn (1962, 1970) that a shift to a cybernetic epistemology is experienced by doctoral students as *a revolution in thinking* comparable to his description of paradigm shifts in the scientific community. Becvar's (1986) representation of Kuhn's Revolution Model is depicted in figure 2, page 24, as a circular (cybernetic) model. Kuhn (1970) likewise recognized the pattern of organized circularity of his viewpoint as "not vicious" and mentioned that his theory was "a useful tool for the exploration of scientific behavior and development" (p. 208). The perimeter of the figure depicts the process and praxis of "Revolutions as Changes of World View" as Kuhn (1962, 1970) described (pp. 111–35). Kuhn (1962, 1970) referred specifically to the pattern of paradigm shift from the historically dominant 17th-century world view of Locke to that of Kant and simple (circular) cybernetics.

Using Kuhn's model as a tool, the inner circle of the illustration (Becvar, 1986) depicts the patterned stages of cybernetic change consistent with Sluzki's (1985) "Minimal Map of Cybernetics" (p.26). Keeney (1983) stated that "cybernetics studies how processes of change determine various *orders* of stability or control" (italics added), (p. 71).

The study of cybernetic patterns of organization distinguishes between simple feedback and higher order feedback processes in which invisible recursion occurs and activates the recursive "order of feedback process that will enable a disturbed ecology to correct itself" (Keeney, 1983, p. 71). Correction requires Second Order Change, which refers

Figure 2. Kuhn's Revolution Model*

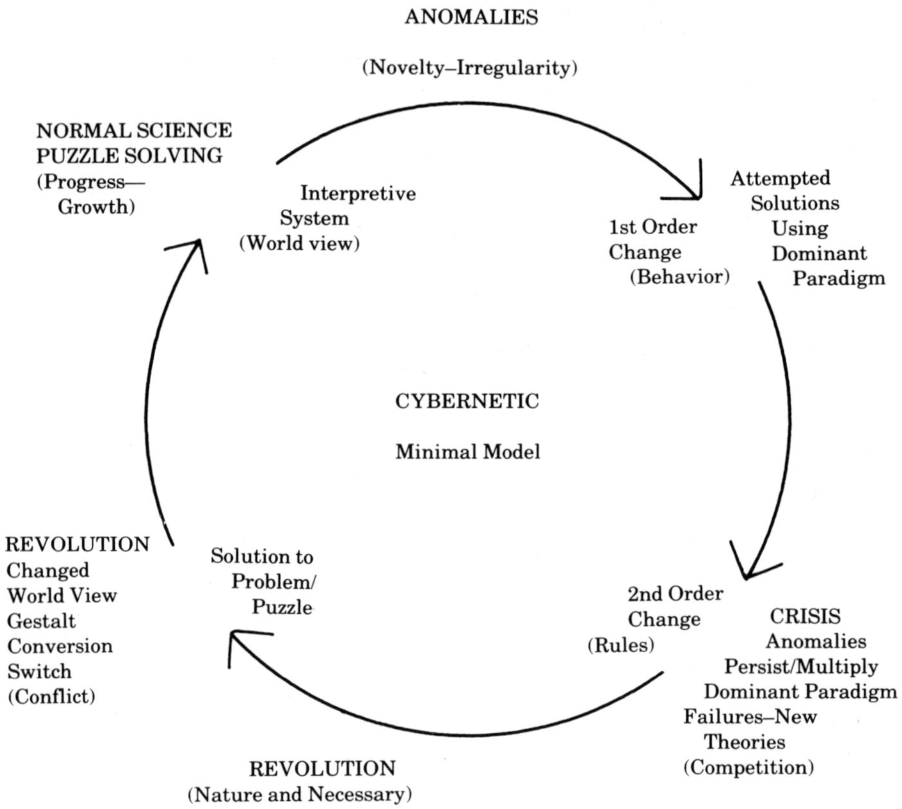

*Becvar, 1986 (classnotes)

to the experience of a change to recursion and meta-cybernetic processes, analogous to a cybernetic epistemology and Bateson's (1972) Learning III change. Still, Kniskern (1983), referring to Kuhn's pattern of circular description of paradigm shift, claimed that "neglecting complex larger *patterns*" leads to a "distorted view of the world" (p. 60).

In the description of Kuhn's Revolution Model (Becvar, 1986), words used in paraphrase remain true to Kuhn's (1962, 1970) text in order to preserve his categorical residual theme and tone of "revolutions as nature and necessity" pattern of organizational process metaphor. Revolutionary change involves the dynamic process of progress through patterned growth and competition, leading to conflict dynamics of "Revolutions as Changes of World View" (pp. 111–35).

Consistent with Kuhn's (1962, 1970) theoretical pattern of process, revolutionary change evolves through four phases. Each of these phases is organized and discussed under separate categorical headings. They include "Normal Science as Puzzle Solving," "Anomalies," "Crisis," and "Revolution." (See figure 2.)

Normal Science as Puzzle Solving: This phase of scientific activity is characterized by Kuhn (1962, 1970) as continual pattern of competition and conflict between various scientific communities. There are a number of distinct views that are roughly compatible with the dictates of scientific observation and methods. However, differences in views are couched in their "incommensurability" perceived irrelevance/dissonance (Festinger, 1957), or inability to be measured against each other. In other words, patterned views seem to share nothing in common and are seemingly always at cross-purpose. To Kuhn, world views are those personal and historical accidents that form a constellation of received beliefs to which the scientific community is committed. Higher educational communities initiate, prepare, and license members in a maturation process that is both rigorous and rigid, thereby gaining a deep hold on the scientific mind. This, according to Kuhn, accounts for the efficiency of normal science as puzzle solving. The direction scientists take in this phase is to immediately firm up answers to universal questions such as:

> What are the fundamental entities of which the universe is composed?
> How do they interact with each other and with the senses?
> What questions may legitimately be asked about such entitles and what techniques employed in seeking solutions?*
>
> [Kuhn, 1962, 1970, p. 5]

**The Structure of Scientific Revolutions* (Chicago: University of Chicago Press, 1962, 1970), © 1962.

Normal science phase research is described as "a strenuous devoted attempt to force nature into conceptual boxes supplied by professional education" (p.5). It is arguable whether science could progress without this "boxing." Paradoxically, this point has an important effect in later revolutionary developments as anomalies build up without a space (conceptual box) to call their own. This normal science phase is a time of activity in puzzle solving. While the dominant paradigm reigns unchallenged, progress is unhampered by "invisible" anomalous buildup and the pattern of "competition and conflict" between scientific communities is viewed as contributive to "progress and growth."

Further, normal science is pictured as an organizing "highly cumulative enterprise eminently successful in its aim, the steady extension of the scope and precision of scientific knowledge" (p.52). Kuhn portrays this phase as the organized "mature" practice of "mopping-up" unsolved puzzles, thereby gaining understanding, prediction, and control. Normal science achieves its goals "predicated on the assumptions that the scientific community *knows* what the world is like" (p. 5). The successes of that community are to a great extent due to the community's remaining willing to defend this structural assumption, at times at considerable cost, "fight rather than switch." Kuhn cited such past "costly" revolutions as those of Copernicus, Newton, and Einstein. Unquestioned commitment to assumptions involves suppression of novelty or anomaly, which is considered "subversive" to progress. Shifting to a new paradigm necessitates community rejection of time-honored theory in favor of another incompatible theory of unknown processes and power.

Anomalies: An anomaly or novelty is a pattern of irregularity, something not understood in terms of the prevailing paradigm, and thus is unpredictable or out of control. Theoretically, anomalies are novelties of fact and/or theory that surface during the phase of normal science puzzle solving. Initially, contradictions to the reigning paradigm are disregarded or ignored for complex patterned philosophical, political, economic, or religious reasons. As long as the dominant pradigm appears to be doing a better job than any other novel concepts threatening violation of its interests, the world acts by tuning them out. There is, in this anomaly phase, a frantic attempt to pound round anomalies into square dominant paradigm holes.

However, Kuhn insists that patterns of novelty or anomaly cannot ultimately be suppressed, due to the arbitrary *either/or* singular demonstrative element of conceptual boxing. Fitting facts to a theory frame is conceptual boxing. When the facts don't fit the frame, there is an "Awareness of something gone wrong . . . [which] does relate" to the effect something has gone wrong before. Awareness of overflow "adjusts conceptual categories" until anomalies become the "anticipated." Suppression and resistance thus serve as the backdrop, paradoxically, "effective in causing them to arise" (p. 64). Discovery, according to Kuhn, involves the following patterned characteristics: (1) previous awareness of anomaly; (2) the consequential change of paradigm categories and processes. This process change of categories is "often accompanied by resistance. There is even evidence that these same characteristics are built into the nature of the perceptual process itself" (p.62). Eventually, the disorganizing dilemma becomes so severe that it leads to the "crisis phase" of the model.

Crisis: Kuhn characterizes this phase as one of "equipment failure," which refers to the acceptance of a pattern of anomaly out of line with expected or predicted results. That is, something repeatedly goes astray and there is a control problem. A pattern of evasion of anomalies only serves to subvert the structure of the dominant paradigm all the more. For anomalies persist and multiply, posing an ever greater threat to the favored paradigm. Usually isolated by its belief and faith in the prevailing tradition, the scientific community resists, seemingly oblivious to the burgeoning crisis of a pattern to technological breakdown. Indeed: "Professionalization leads . . . to an immense restriction of the scientist's vision and to a considerable resistance to paradigm change" (p. 64). The prelude to crisis, however, has to do with the failure of the existing, mostly unarticulated, organizational rules at the core of the dominant paradigm. These rules are unable to accommodate or recognize anomaly as coming from the very structure of the favored paradigm.

Kuhn defines the patterns of "destructive-constructive paradigm changes . . . as overlapping" (p. 66), and as the phase of "proliferation of competing theories . . . concomitant of crisis" (p. 73). Thus extraordinary investigations lead to a new set of commitments and ultimately a new base of operations is established. However, not everyone converts or shifts. Some respond by deserting the field entirely, others stick it out, fighting a predetermined lost battle. There are also those who follow the surviving pattern and "pick up the other end of the stick, . . . a process that involves handling the same bundle of data . . . in a system of relations . . . by giving them different framework." This, Kuhn stated, is similar in pattern to "a change in visual gestalt" (p. 85). This is the *revolution in thinking* called paradigm shift. Finally, Kuhn wrote, "there is a parallel between political [revolutions] and scientific development [which should] no longer be in doubt" (p. 93). Thus the *revolution* is at hand.

Revolution: Kuhn described this phase as one of extraordinary episodes in which the shift to a new set or organized commitments occurs. Revolutions are viewed as patterns of "tradition-shattering complements to the tradition bound activity of normal science" (p. 6). These experiences are conceptualized as linear patterns of "non-cumulative developmental episodes in which an older paradigm is replaced in whole or in part by an incompatible new one" (p. 92); these are the major "turning points" of revolution as shift *(p. 6)*. Developmental episodes transform "the world within which scientific work is done. . . . Such changes, together with the controversies that almost always accompany them, are the defining characteristics of scientific revolutions" *(p. 6)*. Furthermore, "new theory implies a change in the rules governing the prior practice of normal science" (p. 7).

Kuhn's reference to "developmental episodes" reframes the patterns of organization cf revolutions he described as "nature, necessity, invisible, resolutory, and progressive" *(p.iii)*. In addition, the patterned "aimed for transformations" defined by Kuhn's circular model of revolution can go on indefinitely, inasmuch as "an entire arsenal of dichotomies is available" ready and waiting out there *(p. 8)*. Kuhn outlined the later stages of the revolution process as *educative* and *competitive* as the circular pattern nears closure. His organized pattern includes reconstructive talks and action plans that consist of "defining exemplars, translation to understanding, persuasion, conversion and [the necessary praxis] neural-reprogramming." For "the *conversion experience* that I have likened to the gestalt switch remains, therefore at the heart of the revolutionary process" (1970, p. 204).

Ultimately, the revolutionary impact on the organized domain governed by the competing and rejected paradigms effects re-evaluative procedures and alters past conceptualizations of entities answered by the older paradigm. Accomplished is the shift to "the network of theory through which it [science] deals with the world . . . the scientist's world is qualitatively transformed as well as quantitatively enriched" (p. 7). Normal science as puzzle solving closes the gap, sealing itself off, and begins again newly committed to the pattern of competitive re-construction of conceptual boxes to fit nature according to the new paradigm.

Using Kuhn's circular model of the patterns of organization of revolutionary process, a discussion of the elements of a shift to a cybernetic epistemology follows. After defining cybernetics, interpretative system, first order change, second order change, and solution to the problem or puzzle, each is considered.

A discussion of Bateson's (1972) Learning Level changes Zero through IV (pp. 283–306) follows the preview of cybernetics. An illustration and discussion ensues his suggested use of "Binocular Vision" (pp. 69–79). Bateson held that a close-up look at the patterns that connect recursive orders serves to "burst open categories that drive the change of Learning II toward change at Learning Level III" (1972, p. 305).

Emergent Framework—Cybernetic Preview

Cybernetics is defined by Sluzki (1985) as "the science of patterns of organization" (p. 26). "First Order Cybernetics" (Weiner, 1948), according to Sluzki (1985), was entering its developmental "teens" at the time of Kuhn's initial (1962) account of the pattern of paradigm shift and scientific revolution. Kuhn's (1962, 1970) historical/philosophical theory struck the scientific community much like the revolutionary "shot heard round the world" of Emerson's "Hymn Sung at the Completion of the Battle Monument, Concord." *(Bartlett Quotations,* p. 494). The historical context of 1948 was characterized by language reflecting a mechanistic, Lockean, linear, dichotomous world-in-conflict view. As Rosenthal (1984) suggested, historical context can be easily recognized in the language adopted by emerging disciplines lacking a language of their own. In the then anomalous science of cybernetics (Weiner, 1948) the use of patterned mechanistic power words such *First* and *Second Wave* Cybernetics, *escalation, structure* and *strategic* reflect our recent World War II involvement. By contrast, Second Order cybernetics, "The New Cybernetics," evolved during the seventies with a noticeable shift in the patterns of language, logic, and themes toward an organismic, Kantian, cooperative ecological world view.

Patterns of revolutionary shifts described as a "circular model may or may not" reveal the "larger cybernetic picture" (Keeney, 1983, p. 95). A pattern of recursion surfaces and is described under the phase of Second Order change (analogous to the Crisis phase of Kuhn's Revolution Model, Becvar, 1986). Partial views and description prove pragmatic and useful as long as one remembers the patterns as involving the contextual larger picture. The elements of this new epistemology and the phases of the shift are illustrated in figure 3 (p. 30) as follows.

Interpretive System: The interpretive system is analogous to Kuhn's (1970) "constellation of received beliefs" (p. 175). It refers to a belief and/or value system. It is one's epistemology, or *how* one thinks, knows, and decides. A patterned meta-dichotomous constellation of categorical attitudes, beliefs, and values makes up the interpretive system. Becvar and Becvar (1982) states:

Figure 3. Cybernetic Circular Minimal Model*

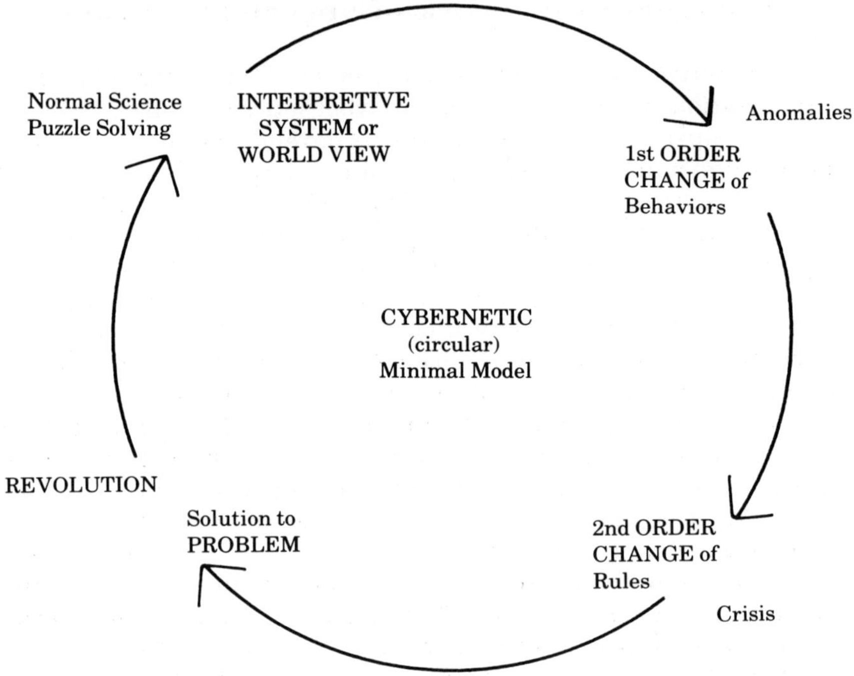

> An interpretive frame can be thought of as containing within it a set of constructs of paired opposites which provide the basis for experiencing meaning for events that occur in the perceptual field. . . . The bi-polar nature of the constructs parallels a positive or negative affective response.
>
> [pp. 28–129]

For example, one views events "outside-in," either "good or bad, cooperative or competitive," et cetera (Becvar and Becvar, 1982, p. 29). Thus what Kuhn (1962, 1970) referred to as "an arsenal of dichotomies" (p. 8) awaits individual interpretation, evaluation, and dissonance of L. II. Much of what goes on in the normal science as puzzle-solving phase goes on between individuals in a patterned process of competition and conflict "predicated on assumptions" that scientists "know" the structural patterns and organization of the world (Kuhn, 1962, 1970, p. 5). Accordingly, patterns of progress and growth are seen as moving toward specific objectives and the categorical "goals" are understanding, prediction, and control. First Order Cybernetics (Sluzki, 1985)

> grew out of communication engineering and computer science as a means of understanding the general principles of how systems of all kinds are regulated . . . based on the assumption that the system being observed can be considered as separate from the observer."
>
> [p. 26]

First order or simple cybernetics "emphasized 'negative' feedback and how systems *maintain* their organization" (p. 26). The focus was mainly on patterned "deviation-countering processes," similar in nature to Kuhn's (1962, 1970) implied repression and "suppression of novelty . . . considered subversive" (p. 64) to progress toward objective goals. Thus the emphasis is on the pattern of organized homeostatis or maintaining stability. "Steady as the goes . . . don't rock the boat . . . " describes this phase of change.

First Order Change: Mindful that phases overlap, first order change refers to a pattern of change within the system while the systems itself remains unchanged. Change is linear and occurs is quantity rather than in quality. The same problem-solving strategies are used over and over again as "new" problems are approached in old ways. If a problem "resists" resolution, a pattern of more old strategies is used and is usually more vigorously applied. "There is either more of a behavior or less . . . along a continuum" (Weeks and L'Abate, 1982, p. 19). Behaviorally, patterns of first order change commonly involve a *shift to the opposite* conceptual type, e.g., passive to aggressive, approach to avoidance, sad to glad, et cetera, or are characterized by an escalation of "more of the same" behavior (Weeks and L'Abate, 1982, p. 19). Thus there is a repetitious pattern of trying different shaped pegs in the same square holes until "awareness" overrides "resistance" to the dilemmas, leading to crisis.

The emergent interest in paradox and an emphasis on change is characteristic of what Sluzki (1985) described as "The Second Wave ('Second Cybernetics') of Maruyama and Magorah (1963)." The second wave appeared during the era in which Kuhn's (1962) paradigm theory was first published.

Second order cybernetics "emphasized 'positive feedback' . . . how systems *change* their organization" (Sluzki, 1985, p. 26); the main emphasis is thus on erratic patterns of deviation-amplifying mechanism processes. These deviation-amplifying tactics paradoxically increase anomalous buildup, leading to crises, and eventually facilitate "revolutionary" reorganized breakthrough. However, a shift to the opposite or same pole behavior invovles an order of recursive patterns of a complementary and/or symmetrical nature; that is, opposite poles "mutually feed and maintain each other" (Becvar and Becvar, 1982, p. 23). Complementary patterns of interaction involve *opposite* kinds of behaviors or "you can't have one without the other." Symmetrical exchanges tend to be behaviors of the *same* or of patterned "one upmanship"; both patterns are interactionally *complete,* recursivly bound to one another. Thus the paradoxical and recursive nature of anomalies and novelty maintain the patterns of paradigm categories and processes. With first order change, so-called solutions maintain problems. In wake of amplified crisis when "the structure of interaction remains constant . . . " (Weeks & L'Abate, 1982, p. 19) the level of change with a pattern of shift is minimal or none. Although shift of pattern occurs within the system (i.e., a pattern of "mood swings"), there is *no change* of the system. Metaphorically, in the next phase there is the call: "Don't give up the ship! ("But it isn't going anywhere!") "Then let's try rocking it!" Patterns of "Deviation-amplifying tactics induce morphogenic processes" (Sluzki, 1985, p.26).

Second Order Change: Weeks and L'Abate (1982) referred to second order change as "a change of the system itself." The system is thus transformed structurally and/or communicationally. Change of this order "tends to be sudden and radical; it represents a quantum jump . . . to a different level of functioning . . . change is discontinuous and qualitative . . . not logically predictable and often appears abrupt, illogical, and unexpected" (p. 19). Similarly, Kuhn's (1962, 1970) theory described the patterns of "destructive-constructive paradigm changes as overlapping" (p. 66), yet as a time of chaos with the "proliferation of theories concomitant of crisis" (p. 74). There is the chaotic willingness to "try something outside" the framework of existing conceptual boxes—even to shift paradigms. Former well-planned solutions have "gone wrong," maintaining or simply shifting so-called "problem" situations. The governing rules need to be "recalibrated and reconstituted" in a different way and "in a qualitative way behaviorally and/or phenomenologically changed" (Weeks and L'Abate, 1982, p. 21). Second order change brings with it a paradigm shift—perceived by some at Learning Level II (problem solving) to be *the* "change" or *the* solution to the problem or puzzle.

Solution to the Problem or Puzzle: This is the *revolutionary* analogous phase of Kuhn's model. This phase signals an "end" of the pattern of revolutionary process of paradigm shift. The individual experiences a "change" in world view similar to the gestalt conversion switch. The previous phase, of second order change, introduced the "awareness" that old solutions *maintain* problems in first order change attempts. Sluzki (1985) clarifies some confusion by explaining: "'First order' and 'second order' denote a logical typing, i.e., the 'second order' cybernetics is *meta* to, and overinclusive of 'first order' cybernetics." Similarly, second order change is meta to and overinclusive of first order change. In addition, Sluzki (1985) explained that while first order cybernetics focused on

> *patterns out there,* second order cybernetics involved a meta step to include the observer's role in constructing the reality being observed. Reality is no longer conceived as independent of an observer's attempts to organize it. The main concepts include recursiveness, self-reflective processes, complexity, and autonomy.,[italics addes] [p. 26]

Keeney (1983) held that "Bateson, Maturana, Varela, and von Foerster bring us [the news] . . . that all living and mental process involves recursion, self-reference, and paradox" (p. 56). Recursion as cybernetic indicates the "order of recycling" synonomous to "double description, drawing a distinction and punctuation." (See glossary.) For example, punctuation is a non-hierarchical higher order of recursion than drawing a distinction. Autonomy is said to be the "highest order of recursion," symbolic of Bateson's (1987) "sacred." Bateson delineated patterned orders of recursion as "Behavior, Context, and Metacontext," modeled as a "Zig-zag ladder of epistemological analysis of classification of Form and description of Process" (cited in Keeney, 1983, p. 41). Recursion is the conceptualization of the paradoxical pattern that comprises two strands forming the "Strange Loopiness" of Hofstader's (1979) triple bonded *Eternal Golden Braid.* In "general, self-referential paradox underlies all observing systems: The observer's observations may include his/her observing" (Keeney, 1983, p. 32). Recursion and the new cybernetics are part of a change in paradigm that reconstructs patterns organizing one's vision of the world. Finally, by contrast with Kuhn's Revolution Model (Becvar, 1986), the circular model resists closure with a description of second order cybernetics. When a pattern of process enfolds on itself, a "circle is not the best way to think of recursion" (Keeney, 1983, p. 58). Study of recursive patterns of organization—the new cybernetics—reveals a "parital arc" (Keeney, 1983, p. 100), a half-picture—the larger whole is reconstructed in the following sections. Paradoxically, a second order change of world view reframes and allows re-construction of one's patterns of viewing the world, as "qualitatively transformed as well as quantitatively enriched" (Kuhn, 1962, 1970, p. 7), thus activating a pattern of higher order feedback processes "that will enable a disturbed ecology to correct itself" (Keeney, 1983, p. 71). Reframed it thereby encourages one toward the pattern of liberating autonomous "excercise of inventing a reality" as described by the constructivist, von Foerster (cited in Segal, 1986, p. xiv).

Emergent Framework—Bateson's Binocular Vision

In the review of the literature thus far, Rychlak's (1981) traditional "frame of theory-construction constructs . . . [his] Lockean versus Kantian models . . . " helps fulfill his stated hope to further a student's understanding and study. Historical/philosophical *traditional* views helped punctuate the category of traditional epistemological roots for this study's *residual* frame: Kuhn's (1962, 1970) "Revolutions as Changes of World View" (pp. 111–135). Kuhn's (1962, 1970) *residual* construct of paradigm shift implies a lateral move, from———to, an all or nothing gestalt switch in thinking. For example, patterns of organized lateral shift of world view from Locke's dominant world view to Kant's opposing view describe a pattern of recursive first order change of behaviors. Bateson (Keeney, 1983) referred to this order of shift as residual "solutions which maintain problems." Similarly, Bateson (Keeney, 1983) has repeatedly cautioned against "seeing circularity and recursion as the all encompassing picture." Accordingly, an *emergent* pattern of world view shift from Locke to Kant is viewed as a "partial arc a sequence of a more encompassing negative feedback process" (p. 72). It is similar process, in nature to Broderick's (1983) pathological "seesawing negative coalitions" (p. 53).

Summing up, "Broader patterns of organization are indeed recursive . . . 'circular and cybernetic' notions are actually partial arcs, of more encompassing patterns" (Keeney, 1983, p. 57). Thus from these descriptions of partial arcs one could picture a pattern of organization of a philosophical "pendulum's polar swing" (Ferguson, 1980, pp. 71–173) from a dominant demonstrative either/or Lockean world view to a Kantian world view based on dialectical both/and reasoning. However, as Kuhn's Revolution Model (Becvar, 1986) implies, as long as Locke's dominant world view has demonstrated it is doing a better job and anomalies remain below crisis level, theoretically the pendulum stays bound to the dominant pole—secured by the overriding paradoxical "meta-double bind" of Locke's "either/or thinking" (Weeks and L'Abate, 1982, p. 43).

Yet, assuming that Kuhn's (1962, 1970) pattern of paradigm shift from the historically dominant 17th-century world view of linear dichotomies to a 20th-century world view of cybernetics represents a signal to shift from a linear to a recursive world view, there is according to Kuhn's Revolution Model (Becvar, 1986) a pattern of anomalous buildup that has reached crisis proportions. The revolution phase involves a (lateral first order cybernetic) shift—a gestalt conversion switch to a cybernetic (Kantian) world view. Therefore, according to the model, first order change to the opposite or complementary polarity indicates a shift that foretells "more of the same" goings on in a different traditional (Kantian) frame. What is envisioned is how first order change involves patterns of "shift" or "partial arcs" which are habitually punctuated as circular and referred to as "cybernetic" processes, thereby, pragamatically neglecting the "complete binding" patterned effects of contextual recursion. Whereas, second order change involves previously ill-defined cybernetic *complete* recursive contextual "whole" processes and praxes.

Bateson (1979) suggested the use of "binocular vision" (pp. 69–79), used by this study to connect in patterns the traditional 17th-century views and cybernetics. Binocular vision reveals a topology of cybernetic patterns of organization (dominant/submissive) as complementarity at a recursive "synthesizing meta-level." Figure 4 (p.36) gives a new cybernetic look to the same separate lists of meta-assumptions of figure 1 of Becvar (1986) (p. 22)—a first order cybernetic look. For complementary (opposite pole) patterns of interaction logically involve first order change (paradigm shift); that is, they are meta to simple circular cybernetic process. Notice that heretofore "invisible" *revolutionary* patterns of organizational recursion allow conflicting *versus* views to become complementary *verses* views.

Figure 4. Lists of Meta-assumptions of 17th-century World Views Using Bateson's Binocular Vision at a Complementary Metalevel

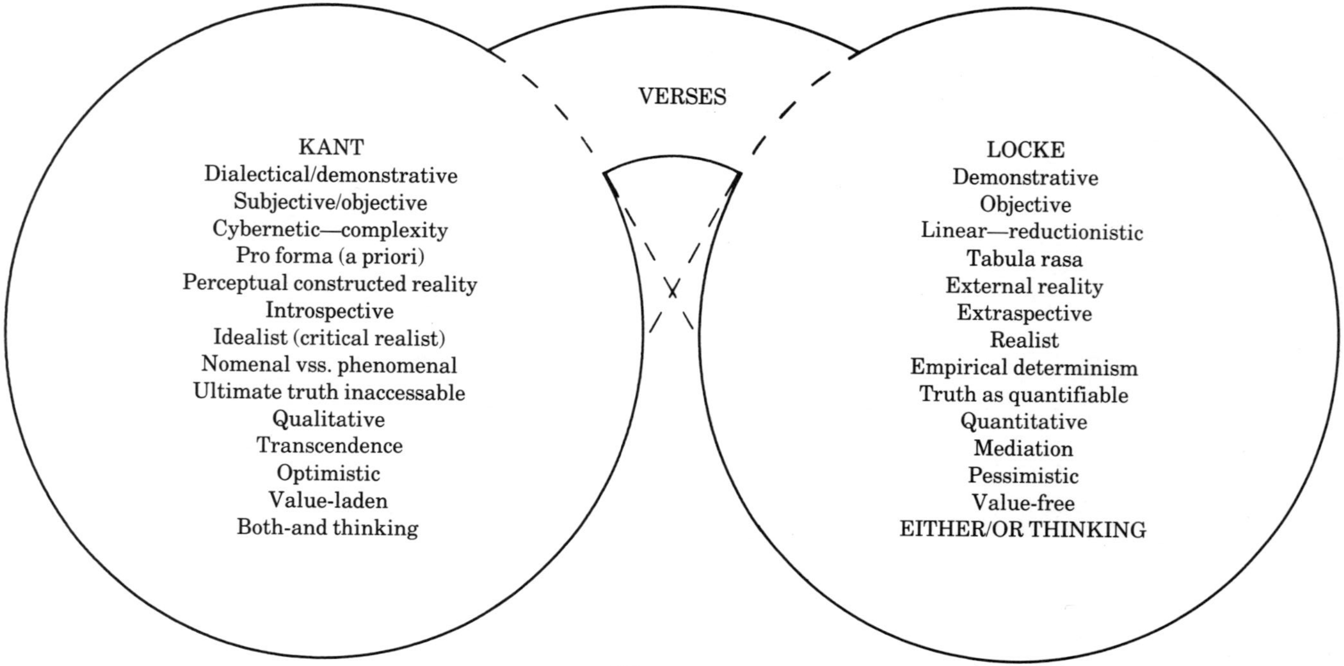

Figure 4's lists of assumptions are the same as figure 1's using a wider perspective of Batesonian (1979) contextual "binocular vision" (p. 131). A "double description" (Keeney, 1983, pp. 37–44) yields an epistemological pattern consistent with a cybernetic of cybernetics look. With a vertical leap to a cybernetic *complementary* meta-level, the patterns of the organization of *versus* views change views to *verses,* or a meta pattern of "you can't have one without the other." Complete systems of polarity "mutually feed and maintain each other" (Becvar and Becvar, 1982, p. 23); what is inferred is that there is a kind of paradoxical pattern of "left-handed," insincere, or dubious *complimentarity* in the organization of traditional and residual world views. Batesonian meta-contextual binoculars "recalibrate and reconstitute" views (Weeks and L'Abate, 1982, p. 21); heretofore invisible patterns of recursive organization complete this dubious *complimentary* picture.

At an objective level Kant and Locke are seen as incompatible opposites, bound by a "complementary" pattern of recursion—with the Lockean world view dominant for close to three centuries, according to Bateson (1979), Keeney (1983), and von Foerster (Segal, 1986). In addition, Bateson (cited in Keeney, 1983) argued personality theories (Rychlak, 1981), psychoanalysis, behaviorism, and phenomenological premises based on dynamics of a conflict paradigm "belong in the same [Lockean] world view" (p. 12). He claimed at a meta-level of complementarity of opposites they become sides of the same "revolutionary" vintage coin (Bateson, 1979; Keeney, 1983, p. 70).

Seventeenth-century and revolutionary epistemology unfolds as a circular patterned Game Without End. This kind of game has lasted for nearly three centuries and has been played with invisible rules of recursion, self-reference, and paradox until anomalies build to crisis proportions and revolutions occur. For patterns of organization as described in *Change* (1974) revealed that

> change of something into its opposite . . . is no change in the overall *pattern*. . . . A system which may run through all its possible internal changes (no matter how many there are) without effecting a systemic change, i.e., second-order change, is said to be caught in a *Game Without End*
>
> [italics added] [Watzlawick, Weakland, and Fisch, 1974, p. 22]

In figure 4 (p. 36), Bateson's (1979) binocular vision was imagined as coupled with Becvar's and Becvar's (1982) reciprocal "lazy-eight" form, represented below. It is useful to illustrate "a pattern that connects" recursive processes that infold on itself. Accordingly, it helped to "move us to a reciprocal [recursive] or circular notion of causality." As Becvar and Becvar (1982) described,

> the systems perspective therefore moves us away from linear cause-effect thinking, i.e., that A influences B but B does not influence A. . . . The systems perspective moves us to a reciprocal or circular notion of causality, i.e., A and B are in dynamic interaction.
>
> [p. 7]

Also, Weeks and L'Abate (1982) had described a scholarly/study resolution of the hold on thinking in patterns of recursive "paradoxical either/or meta-double-binds," of Logical Learning Level II:

> A historical [philosophical] analysis helped to explain much current thinking about problems, thinking which is still primarily linear and interactional. . . . From a dialectical viewpoint, problems are the result of not being able to resolve a thesis-antithesis dilemma because of fixed rules of problem solutions which *bind* the individual to one view of reality.
>
> [italics added] [p. 53]

Bateson implied the scope of L. II's dilemmas: in 1987 Bateson and Bateson wrote "there are so many double-binds in nature they cannot be counted" (p. 204). From the theory of logical types Bateson (1972) charted the following Learning levels of change as

> *ZERO LEARNING* is characterized by *specificity of response*, which—right or wrong—is not subject to correction [Lockean demonstrative reasoning].
>
> LEARNING I is change in *specificity of response* by correction of errors of choice within a set of alternatives [1st order change].
>
> *LEARNING II* is change in the process of Learning I, e.g., a corrective change in the set of alternatives from which choice is made, or it is a change in how the sequence of experience is punctuated [chronic dissonance].
>
> *LEARNING III* is *change in the process of Learning II*, e.g., a corrective change in the system of *sets* of alternative from which choice is made. (. . . to demand this level of performance of some . . . is sometimes pathogenic) [cybernetic shock and second and/or third order change].
>
> *LEARNING IV* would be change in *Learning III*, but probably does

> not occur in any adult living . . . on this earth. . . . The combination of phylogenesis with ontogenesis in fact, achieves Level IV ["Sacred"].
> [p. 293]

Bateson claimed that knowledge of Learning II paradoxical "contraries or double-binds [cognitive dissonance] drive[s]" some people toward "dangerous waters" involved in Learning III, the essence of *cybernetic shock* and epistemology. For example, in language patterns *complementary* and *complimentary* sound the same—this might be one "gap or loophole" charted by Bateson (1972, 1979, 1987). (Note "misspelling" of this nature in "Pro-Log," which is included in the front matter of this volume.) An inference that may serve to "burst open" the categories of recursive contraries that bind one to Learning II-yet drive one to Learning III (p. 303).

Complementary and *complimentary* carry different connotations. They denote profound difference of meaning in processes. To complete, on one hand, or to compliment, on the other, implies very different levels of interactional patterns of recursive process (Fullerman, E., "Mispronunciations," *St. Louis Post-Dispatch,* February, 1988). Complementarity might well be a form of *left-handed complimentarity,* involved in a contextually organized paradoxical meta double-bind Game Without End, an example of a possible gap or loophole to L. III. "Nature" according to Bateson and Bateson (1987) "is a double-binding bitch" (p. 146). The following section attempts to enlarge these "too many to count" contrary conceptualizations (Bateson and Bateson, 1987, p. 204).

Emergent Framework—Cybernetic Epistemology

The foregoing minimal model preview of cybernetics (figure 3, p. 30), the accounts and illustrations of Bateson's binocular vision, and a pattern that connects (like that of Becvar and Becvar, 1982, pp. 7, 29) (figure 4, p. 36) rehearsed a shallow

> plunge into [the deep inner-circle pool of cybernetic epistemology] what Weber called the "tremendous confusion of interdependent influences" and come out not only unconfused but possessed of a clear conception of at least some segment of the web of relations. . . . Warned only "the best scientific minds" would be able to sustain such "continued speculative effort" . . . "the whole system" has been too much to imagine,
> [cited in Rosenthal, 1984, p. 192].

This section of the literature review begins by first anchoring the theoretical assumptions associated with the thesis of this study; (1) A pattern of shift to cybernetic epistemology is accompanied first by cognitive dissonance (Festinger, 1957) that is comparable to Kuhn's (1962, 1970) description of paradigm shifts in the scientific community. This shift is experienced as a *revolution* in thinking. (2) Next there comes the beginning of the shock of cybernetic complexity, of Bateson's (1972) Learning II eternal contraries. As so, descriptions of cybernetic epistemology are considered. The descriptions considered include those of Bateson (1972, 1979, 1987) and Keeney (1983) and the constructs of Varela (1976) and von Foerster (1963, 1978) that von Foerster said were "invented" by Segal (1986). Keeney (1983) portrayed two Epistemologists engaged in dialogue concerning the definition of cybernetic epistemolgy. In the process the definition is further clarified: it "is neither a map, description, model, paradigm nor paradigm of paradigm . . . it is [patterned] process of knowing, constructing and maintaining a world of experience" (pp. 107–108).

Cognitive Dissonance

Reynolds (1971) described Festinger's (1957) theory of cognitive dissonance (a form of Kuhn paradigm variation, pp. 38–39) that is hypothesized as involved with Bateson's (1972) Learning Level II "contraries, contradictions and double-binds" and "the fact of reversal" (pp. 302–303) or as "left-handed compliments". Learning III involves *cybernetic shock* and the learning level processes and praxes of becoming cybernetic epistemologists. Reynolds (1971) described cognitive dissonance as having three differing states: (1) cognitions that "fit" logically together are said to be *consonant;* (2) cognitions that "compete or conflict," that logically do not fit, are said to be *dissonant;* (3) cognitions that logically lack any relevance with each other are said to be *irrelevant,* bearing no relationship. The assumptions involved is that patterned cognitions should fit or be consonant or that cognitions that are perceived as irrelevant "should" (Ellis, 1975, p. 218) remain distant and unrelated. There is, in either of these instances, the decided assumption that one *should* know "either/or" *how* the world is organized. Cognitive dissonance followed by cybernetic shock occurs when one's pragmatic world view lacks consonance and complex patterns of objective reality become relevant and relative. Dissonance, therefore, involves *shoulds* that are experienced as confusing, uncomfortable, tense concerns about one's "objective" patterned view of the world—not fitting "reality" (Ellis, 1975, pp. 177–85). According to cognitive theory (Ellis, 1975, pp. 11–12) the individual takes action either to change world views (shift) or change *HOW* s/he views the world—or "suffer" the "neurotic" consequences of chronic dissonance at Learning Level II ("Damning self, others and/or the world" [Ellis, 1975, p. 33]).

Kuhn (1962, 1970) similarly related the dissonant experience of shifting paradigms posing this question: "How do scientists proceed when aware only that something has gone wrong at a *level* with which their training has not equipped them to deal?" (p. 112.) Objectively he told of the experience and perception of doctoral students, as research subjects, involved in the phenomenon of *revolutionary* paradigm shift:

> At the start his perceptual apparatus functions as it had been trained to function . . . the result is extreme disorientation, an acute personal crisis. But after the subject has begun to learn to deal with his new world, his entire visual field flips over, usually after an intervening period in which vision is simply confused. The assimilation of a previously anomalous visual field has reacted upon and changed the field itself. Literally as well as metaphorically, the man . . . had undergone a revolutionary transformation of vision.
>
> [p. 112]

And so, Festinger's (1957) theory of cognitive dissonance is anchored alongside Kuhn's (1962, 1970) "telling" experience of the "revolutionary transformation of vision" (p. 112) of research subjects and/or doctoral students. *Cybernetic shock is the confusion and concern over complex recursive patterns of organization.* A related question on dissonance and "the fact of reversal" was posed by Bateson (1979), which characteristically broadens perspective. He asked: "Why do schools teach almost nothing of the [recursive] patterns which connect?" (p. 8.) In a relatively lengthy narrative, he took on some of the major assumptions of Newtonian epistemology, which are consonant and historically involve a broader study of theoretical assumptions of the 17th-century world view of Locke (Burke, 1985, pp. 175–76). In fact, Becvar's (1986) lists of 17th-century assumptions (figure 1) originally involve Newton, Descartes, Aristotle, and Bacon as parts of the dominant paradigm network. This narrative of Bateson's (1979) bears repeating since it addresses the metastability of Lockean exemplars and current traditional and residual educational policies:

> At the meeting of the Committee on Education Policy, July 20, 1978, I remarked that current educational processes are a "rip-off," from the point of view of the student. . . . It is a matter of obsolescence . . . I refer

> to such notions as: a) The *Cartesian dualism* separating "mind, and matter." b) The strange *physicalism* of the *metaphors* which we use to describe and explain mental phenomena—"*power,*" "*tension,*" "*energy,*" "*social forces,*" etc . . . c) Our anti-aesthetic assumptions, borrowed from the emphasis which *Bacon, Locke,* and *Newton* long ago gave to the physical sciences, viz. that all phenomena (including mental processes) can and shall be studied and evaluated in *quantitative* terms. . . . The view of the world—the latent and partly unconscious epistemology—which such ideas together generate is out of date . . . pragmatically, ... intellectually . . . [and] As a base for religion . . . [was] clearly intolerable and obsolete about a hundred years ago. . . . [italics added].*
>
> [pp. 217–18]

Then as his daughter, Catherine Bateson (1985), affectionately wrote, speaking of her father's cybernetic thinking/writing: "he putts-along and writes, 'It is not so much 'power' that corrupts as the *myth*—of 'power.' . . . *physical metaphors* are to be distrusted . . . [and are] dangerous" (p. 45). Her father had the last word, ending the earlier narrative with "The wider perspective is about perspectives . . . Do we . . . foster . . . promote in students . . . that which will bring our system back into an appropriate synchrony or harmony between rigor [objectivity] and imagination [subjectivity]. As teachers, are we wise?" (Bateson, 1979, p. 223.)

The significance of Bateson's (1979) quotation is that it addressed the exemplars of the 17th-century world view of Locke (figures 1, 4 and 5). Bateson (1979) inferred the patterns of "obsolescence" of exemplars involved with the traditionally dominant world view of Locke, signaling that perhaps a lateral paradigm shift to a Kantian world view is needed—or another recycling around what Bateson (1979) called a circular "evolutionary cul-de-sac" (p. 208) with Locke's complement, Kant, at the wheel. Surprisingly, it seems to neglect a vertical leap of second order cybernetic synthesis—where larger patterns of recursion, self-reference, complexity and, meta to these, autonomy, and the "sacred" lie. According to Keeney (1983) autonomous processes are the highest order of recursion involving generation and *maintainance* of the whole (p. 84).

Theoretically pertinent is the cybernetic epistemological connections involving Bateson, Keeney, von Foerster, Varela, and Maturana. Keeney (1983) dedicated his account of *The Aesthetics of Change* to Gregory Bateson; its foreword was written by Heinz von Foerster, a constructivist, involved in the next section of the literature review, "Cybernetics and Beyond." In the chapters Keeney (1983) wrote on the "Fundamentals of Epistemology," and "Cybernetic Epistemology," he too relied heavily on the past thinking/writings of these notables in cybernetics and related fields. Keeny's synthesis and overlap of their patterns of "parallel" cybernetic thinking and writings make analysis difficult—to quote Weber (cited in Rosenthal, 1984); "only 'the best scientific minds' would be able to sustain such 'continued speculative effort' . . . the whole system has been too much to imagine" (p.192).

Keeney's (1983) representations are credited as aesthetic by von Foerster, and accordingly (p. xi), in Segal's (1986) *The Dream of Reality,* von Foerster said that his constructs bear more coherence than Bateson's. Paradoxically, von Foerster, while "commenting on Bateson's [characteristic] style of giving puzzling and mystifying answers to simple clear questions . . . I [von Foerster] opened a presentation, [Bateson attending] entitled 'Contradictions, Paradoxes, Vicious Circles, and other Creative Devices'" (p. xiii). Keeney's (1983) aesthetic view of a cybernetic epistemology described how important it is "to realize that an understanding of cybernetic epistemology may completely alter one's habits of action. . . . Furthermore, the deepest order of change that human beings are capable of demonstrating is epistemological change . . . [Learning III] transforming one's way of experiencing the world" (p. 6). He continued: "To enter the world of cybernetic thought . . . [constructs] a radically different world view." He cautioned, however, that the world of transition is a fuzzy one. . . . We are, therefore, caught in a state of transition . . . caught between two "realities" [poetically]

> Wandering between two worlds, one dead, the other powerless to be born . . .
>
> [Arnold, 1855/1973, p. 608; Kenney, 1983, p. 16]

Keeney (1983) then offered, aesthetically, that "hope still remains . . . .cybernetic epistemology provides the path." Finding the path, paradoxically, requires

> "a condition of complete simplicity
> (costing not less than everything)
> And all shall be well." (T. S. Eliot,
> 1943/1973, p. 59; Keeney, 1983, p. 11).

Bateson (1972) recounted, "Cybernetics is the biggest bite of the fruit of the Tree of Knowledge that mankind has taken in the last 2000 years" (p. 476). The cybernetic view gestures, seemingly beyond the gestalt conversion of Kuhn's (1962, 1970) paradigm shift, and meta even to first order change of complementarity or synthesis of 17th-century world views. In Keeney's (1983) portrayal of cybernetic epistemology we are drawn "toward seeing a world that by definition is impossible to grasp in the world to which one is traditionally accustomed" (p. 11).

The cybernetic epistemolgist's view presents what Bateson (1979) termed "the difference, that makes a difference ('information'), required in order to interrupt the recursive dance between [Lockean] form and [Kantian] process" (p. 99). For Bateson related that "unchecked *symmetry* or *complementarity* [italics added] led to 'schismogenesis' . . . intolerable stress and dissolution" (cited in Keeney, 1983, pp. 39–40). Bateson's schismogenesis parallels Rollo May's (1969) description of "Our Schizoid World" (pp. 13–36).

Keeney (1983) described the difficulty of staying afloat in cybernetic epistemological waters. Upon touching ground, he directs: "The starting point . . . is therefore an observer drawing distinction in order to observe . . . [and to] punctuate the sequence of events" (p. 24). As his dialoguing Epistemologists again held forth: "There is nothing (in living and mental process) but self-reference, recursion and paradox" (p. 56). He revealed how "the trick is to re-cognize patterns . . . recursive or cybernetic . . . [thus,] acknowledge that we always have been cybernetic epistemologists" (p. 60). The trick is in knowing.

Keeney (1983) related that it was Margaret Mead (1968) who first suggested the meta pattern of "cybernetics of cybernetics" as second order recursion "placing the observer in, as a part of the observations made" (p. 76) (subjective/objectivity). Keeney (1983) further specified description as self-reference and as an error of objectivity, assuming "a separation of the observer and the observed" (p. 78). According to von Foerster (cited in Keeney, 1983), "subjective statements are made by subjects . . . objective statements are made by objects . . . too bad these damned things don't make any statements" (p. 79). Keeney (1983) went on to describe this (subjective/objective) first order of recursion as complementary, because implying that objectivity is nonsensical suggests that "subjectivity is also nonsense" (p. 80). Keeney (1983) gave another clue circling back to 17th-century world views, seeing "Kant as the initiator of this shift and . . . [how] this paradigmatic change replaces our concern with objectivity to one of *responsibility*" (p. 81) for re-structuring one's patterns of organizational processes.

Cybernetics of cybernetics sets forth a basic form for release from the paradoxical meta–double-bind of either/or thinking and the recursive dance of complementarity/symmetry. Varela (cited in Keeney,

1983) defined a formula of: "the it"/"the process leading to it" (p. 94).

To apply this formula; Varela wrote that one must "take any situation (domain, process, entity, notion) which is holistic (total, closed, complete, full, stable, self-contained). Put [this] on the left side of the '/.' Put on the right side of it the corresponding processes constituents, generators, dynamics" (p. 94). "Being/becoming," is the essence of the process. For example: "being Ph.D."/"is the process of becoming Ph.D." Or "being a cybernetic epistemologist"/"is the process of becoming a cybernetic epistemologist."

Cybernetic complementarity deals with first order of recursion. For example, Bateson (1979) punctuates: (1) behaviors as first order recursion (simple cybernetics); (2) context as second order recursion (cybernetics of cybernetics); (3) and meta-context as "self-referential" autonomy, as "the highest order of recursion" (cybernetics of cybernetics of cybernetics). *Higher* orders are depicted in a non-hierarchical sense; "such depictions are 'artifacts' " (Keeney, 1983, p. 46–47). Further examples involve complementarity/symmetry (objectivity) patterns as first order recursion, as simple circular cybernetics. Context, on the other hand, involves second order recursion (subjective/objectivity) or cybernetics of cybernetics. Meta-context, the highest order of recursion, involves "both/and" or autonomy of the whole *complete* closure of the system—patterned as cybernetics of cybernetics of cybernetics. Bateson (1979) described this mode as a "dialectical zig-zag ladder" for analysis involving both "form and process" (pp. 194–95). Similarly, Keeney (1983) described how "simple cybernetics and cybernetics of cybernetics are [in themselves] halves of a cybernetic complementarity" (p. 101). See figures 1, 4, and 5.)

Varela also believed that complementary opposites, symmetrical escalation or dualisms, are summed up as only half the picture or simple circular cybernetic first order recursion. "The larger cybernetic picture is that the [revolutionary] battle [overt or covert] is a means or process of generating, maintaining and stabilizing an ecosystem" (cited in Keeney, 1983, pp. 93–94). Broadening this perspective, in symmetry and/or complementary/objectivity, first order recursive processes are simple cybernetics (Bateson's behavioral order). Applying Varela's formula:

1st order:	(behavioral) complementary/symmetrical
2nd order:	context/imagination/rigor
or	context/power/submission

First order behavioral descriptions neglect higher orders of recursion. Behavioral simple cybernetic descriptions represent half the picture, the right side of the "/"—the *left side* corresponds to contextual processes, "constituents, generators, and dynamics"—yielding a recursive cybernetics of cybernetics of cybernetics meta-picture. In other words, applying Varela's formula once again, generates a meta-level pattern look at both 17th-century world views placed on the right side of the "/" (simple cybernetic complementarity), with Varela's construct of the *revolutionary "battle* is a means or process of generating, maintaining, and stabilizing an ecosystem" on the *left* (cybernetics of cybernetics complementarity). To illustrate:

Meta-Revolutions	/	Revolutions
"the battle is a means or process of generating, maintaining, and stabilizing an ecosystem" (p. 94). (complementarity at the recursive second order of cybernetics of cybernetics)	/	LOCKE / KANT (complementarity at the recursive first order of simple cybernetics)

In a reflective manner, it is in moving from the traditional frame (17th-century world views, Figure 1) through the residual frame (Kuhn's Revolution Model [Becvar, 1986], Figure 2) and into the meta-emergent frames (Cybernetic Epistemology and Cybernetics and Beyond) that Bateson (1979), again, characteristically, helps muddy the waters, involving construction of two disturbing metaphors that transform thinking. (1) The first metaphorical image relates to the objective Kant versus Locke lists of meta-assumptions (Figure 1, p. 22). Versus views split worlds at an objective level. These apparently opposite views were first snared by the partially visible paradoxical meta–double-bind of either/or thinking of Locke's demonstrative world view. Figure 4 (p. 36) found them caught in a gigantic "schismogenic" double-bind at a first order complementary recursive level. Both figures are simple cybernetic discriptions at a behavioral level. Both descriptions fail the test of cybernetics of cybernetics—lacking contextual order. Both versus and verses views neglect the big picture, i.e., the author's *left-handed complimentarity* factor. Visions of "contexts of contexts" reveal "a loophole" to Learning III through which the impact of contradictions can be reduced—bypassing double-binds Bateson (1972) held—bind one at Learning II and chronic dissonance (p. 304). (2) The other metaphor Bateson (1979) described relates to Becvar's (1986) Kuhn's Revolution Model (Figure 2, p. 24), as is referred to in the introduction to this study (page 15): Bateson (1979) explained to his daughter how "any species can get into an evolutionary cul-de-sac . . . be a party to its own extinction" through competition leading to conflict. (p. 208). In agreement, this metaphor reflects the pattern of confusion and concern or *cybernetic shock* of the author and respondents: a cul-de-sac has only one entry—which is its only exit—how many *Revolutions* before the "outer-limits" of circularity are irreparably violated? (Bateson, 1979, p. 208.) Similarly imaged is the mythical Ouroboros that nurtures itself by consuming its own tail; there seems ominous ends to the orders of infinite recycling process (Keeney, 1983, p. 32). Imagined, Becvar and Becvar's (1982) lazy-eight form clearly illustrates the bigger picture of "left-handed complimentarity" described (p. 7). Kuhn's Revolution Model (Becvar, 1986) is imaged in a similar manner. Somehow, these whole visions or versions do not make a pretty picture. (See p. 48.) Fraser (1984) agreed and went as far as to hold that "Corrective Vision for a Binocular View" is not so "enriching but enraging . . . once [meta] vicious cycles are seen, [furthermore] it is difficult not to try to interrupt them" (p. 46). In agreement, Bateson (1979) and Keeney (1983) also held they are "vulgar power issues" (p. 27). Segal (1986), like Bateson and Keeney, held that by pragmatically "punctuating circular streams of interaction into one-way causalities . . . [one is] unwittingly seduced into habitual causal schemes for explaining the world" (p. 58). Perhaps these words of "Bateson (cited by M. C. Bateson, 1972)" give another clue, that is, "rigor [objectivity] alone is paralytic death but imagination [subjectivity] alone is insanity" (schismogenic). Yet Keeney (1983) insisted: "The aesthetic quest necessarily involves a recursive dance between rigor and imagination" (p. 94).

In other words, circular description are simple cybernetic processes that thereby neglect, yet reflect, what Kuhn (1962, 1970) implied as a basic tenent of waging "Invisible Revolutions" (p. 136). Cybernetic of cybernetic complementarity/symmetry of larger contextual interaction cannot be seen using circular description. Figure 5 (p. 00) presents the author's earlier described images: a big picture—meta–contextually inclusive—autonomous, in essence. These following patterned illustrations re-present the re-construction of form, process, and the patterns of organization that connect thus far: (1) versus views or those of competition and conflict, (2) Bateson's synthesizing binocular vision, (3) Varela's "/" larger picture, and (4) the lazy-eight pattern that connects of Becvar and Becvar (1982, p. 7). These "Bootstrapper" illustrations show how "patterns do not 'contain' one another, rather they 'involve' one another" (Chew cited in Capra, 1985, p. 94).

The following section, "Cybernetics and Beyond," considers *emergent and beyond* views, a symbolic step beyond traditional/ residual/ emergent frames, and proceeds to explore patterns of organization overarching the triad of conceptual frameworks. The science of cybernetic

Figure 5. Application of Varela's Larger Picture

Formula Applied to Lockean and Kantian World Views

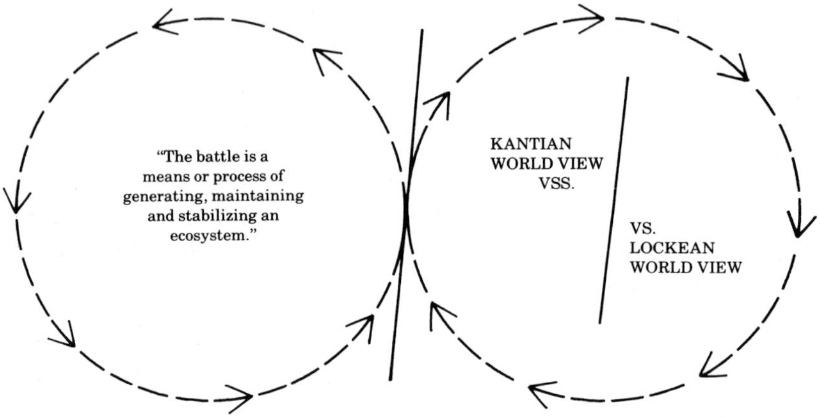

Formula Applied to Kuhn's Revolution Model

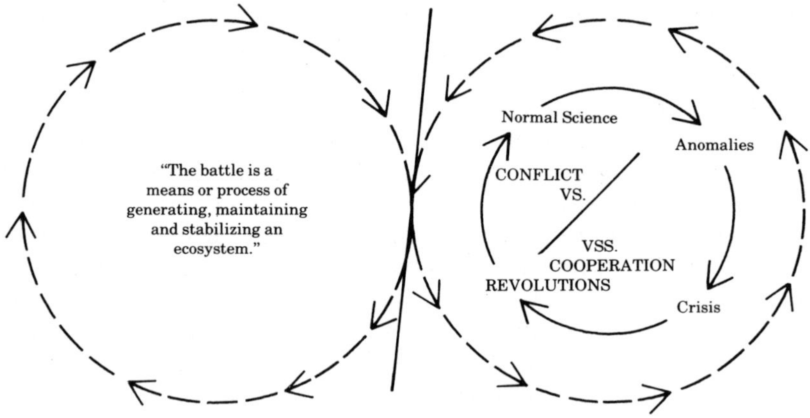

(Invisible recursion)

Derived from Becvar and Becvar (1982).

patterns of organization and the philosophy of *how we think, know, and decide—epistemology*—merge in the beyond territory of contemporary universal views of the last decade. The patterns that bind ideas together "are as close as we can get to ultimate truth" (Bateson, 1979, p. 191).

Cybernetics and Beyond

Universal Co-evolutional Views

The background and problem statements of this study indicate that this review of the literature should end with second order cybernetics, the *natural* recursive nature of world view (Learning II). That, however, would end the review with only half of the picture. The findings from application of Varela's formula for viewing "the larger picture" of shifting paradigms (Locke/Kant)—the contextual left-handed complimentary revolutionary "battle [as] a means or process of generating, maintaining, and stabilizing an ecosystem"—enlarges the scope of patterned late–20th-century contextual dynamics.

Theoretically is seems required that the duality Locke and Kant continue to repetitiously triage, in patterns of: *generate, maintain, stabilize*—generate, maintain, stabilize . . . ad infinitum, *revolutions* as change of world views, based on the value system of competition and conflict, progress and growth. Both views are useful AND a solid philosophical theoretical basis of a different nature and attitude (cooperation and ethical tolerance). A paradigm of universal co-evolution—meta-inclusive of world views—constructs an image of an equilateral arrangement, with Locke, Kant, and co-evolution serving as the three sides of a "therapeutic triangle" (Broderick, 1983).

"Mysterious" triads of events called "stimulus, response, and reinforcement" were implied with laboratory learning (Bateson and Bateson, 1987). The triadic pattern is bonded together by reinforcement attached to value labeling (right/wrong, good/bad). Reinforcement is seen as the evaluative (verbal and/or non-verbalized) comment on the relationship "between" two or more events punctuated in a sequence. Identification of different parts of triads depends on and is subject to various distortions and varies from person to person. Persons evaluate and "impose upon their world the premise that 'right' and 'wrong' are attributes of items rather than of relations between . . . " (pp. 47–48).

Earlier, Bateson (1979) wrote of "the combination of diverse pieces of information" as an "approach of very great power to what I call the pattern which connects . . . insight develops from the comparison of sources, [thereby] throws light on how the universe is integrated." The "bonus" may lead to the "ultimate goal in an inquiry into the *larger pattern which connects"* (p. 68). For example, subatomic physics (Jones and Wilson, 1987) implicates how "opaque or invisible entitles called quarks and their elementary particles arrange themselves in *triangles.*" Quarks *couple* with other quarks and the environment "in such standard combinations as protons (two up quarks and a down quark), neutrons (two down quarks and an up quark). "Scientists recognize that the patterns of " . . . quarks pack a mean intellectual wallop . . . They imply that nature is *three-sided,* and that such *dualistic constructions* as time/space, mind/body and *either/or* miss the point . . . " Quarks represent "Specks of infinity on the one hand, building blocks of the universe on the other, quarks represent science at its most ambitious—also its coyest" (pp. 479–180).

And so the patterns of "Triads and their qualities have been studied from many points of view . . . a three-sided relationship is different in many crucial ways from a dyad or a larger group . . . after generations of partisan conflict . . . [left-handed complimentarity] [the task] is to overcome negative coalitions" or *battling dyads* (Broderick, 1983, p. 13). Figure 6, page 53 illustrates the use of "therapeutic triangulation" to overcome negative coalitions by introducing a "different" third universal view, thereby relaxing the recursive meta–double-bind of paradoxical either/or (dyadic) thinking. Its legend explains the patterned process of "congruent triangulation."

In the same triadic frame, Ford (1975) described Polak's (1961) patterned "metaphysical image of an eye in a triangle, as a'mystical model' of time," symbolically representing the "past, present and future" at the intersect. Congruently, the vertices of the medians of the triangle overlie the center of the circle (as in figure 6, p. 53), representative of "the eye at the intersect" the image point of "a making moment" (p. 432), the congruent "Zenith" point; Bateson's (1987) "ECO"-logical "sacred" view (p. 145).

Scarf (1987), similar to Bateson's pattern concept of infinite double-binds in nature, described how "Transient Triangles" abound "in the everyday world." Triangulation allows a "tense twosome" to skirt sensitive issues. "Navigating around them counters change for better or worse"; the twosome brings up a third issue (or person) to stabilize the "natural" (complementary/symmetrical) recursive instability of dyads. Dyads are like two-legged tables—naturally difficult to balance—a three-legged table or "a tripod provides a secure base" (pp. 245—146); a tripod bronze altar gave sustenance to the sacred Oracle at Delphi when responding to philosophical dilemma. *(Encyclopedia Americana,* vol. 27 [1961], p. 74). Triangulation is a well-advised move if it's therapeutically flexible and dynamic.

Indeed, Rychlak (1981) patterned Bandura's "actual schematization construct of reciprocity" as an equilateral triangle (p. 778). Bandura said,

> In the social learning view, behavior, cognitive and other personal factors and environmental influences all operate as interlocking determinants of one another. . . . Within each of the triadic factors there exist, of course, many reciprocal processes. In the action domain, particular movements reciprocally activate other movement patterns. Similarly, there exist reciprocal [symmetrically] spiraling processes . . . The occurrence of an environmental event likewise reciprocally affects other environmental events.
>
> [p. 782]

Then the architectural triangle has been called the most stable structure constructed *(Encylcopedia International,* vol. 18, [1980], p. 218); Bowen (cited in Guerin, 1976) specified the stucture of "The triangle is the smallest stable relationship system . . . a two-person system may be stable as long as it is calm . . . [but] when tension [crisis] . . . is too great . . . it involves others to become *a series of interlocking triangles"* (p. 76).

Keeney's (1983) Epistemologist tells how "lineal" thinking makes sense as long as it is remembered that "partial arcs" are only a part of a

> more encompassing pattern of circularity. . . . Forgetting about broader patterns is what gets us in trouble. . . . There is no reason to throw away plane geometry. Who could build a tennis court without the flat earth hypotheses? . . . realize there is no such thing as a circular or recursive epistemology that bans so-called lineal thinking.
>
> [pp. 56–57]

A flexible "transient therapeutic triangle" pattern represents what Bateson (1979) suggested as a useful "method of double or multiple comparison. . . . [It creates] an extra demension called depth . . . a display inviting the reader to achieve insight by comparing the instances one with another" in essence called the "*manner of search* of the science called 'epistemology.' Epistemology is an individual, integrated meta-science of mind in the widest sense" (p. 87). Bateson (1979) alluded to the processes of triangulation as follows:

Equilateral triangle:

Any of the sides may be considered the base . . . the three points of intersect are vertices . . . the lengths of the lines joining are the sides . . . three sides and three angles are the six parts . . . the perpendicular distance from one to the bases to its opposite vertex is the altitude . . . the line segment joining the midpoint of a side to the opposite vertex is the median . . . all three altitudes go through a single point, and all three medians go through a single (usually different) point . . . all three angles are the same . . . the sum of the angles is exactly equal to two right angles . . . if two triangles are congruent . . . any three independent parts of one are the same as the corresponding three parts of the other." *(Columbia Encyclopedia,* 2 ed. [1950] p. 2008).

Figure 6. Therapuetic Triangulation

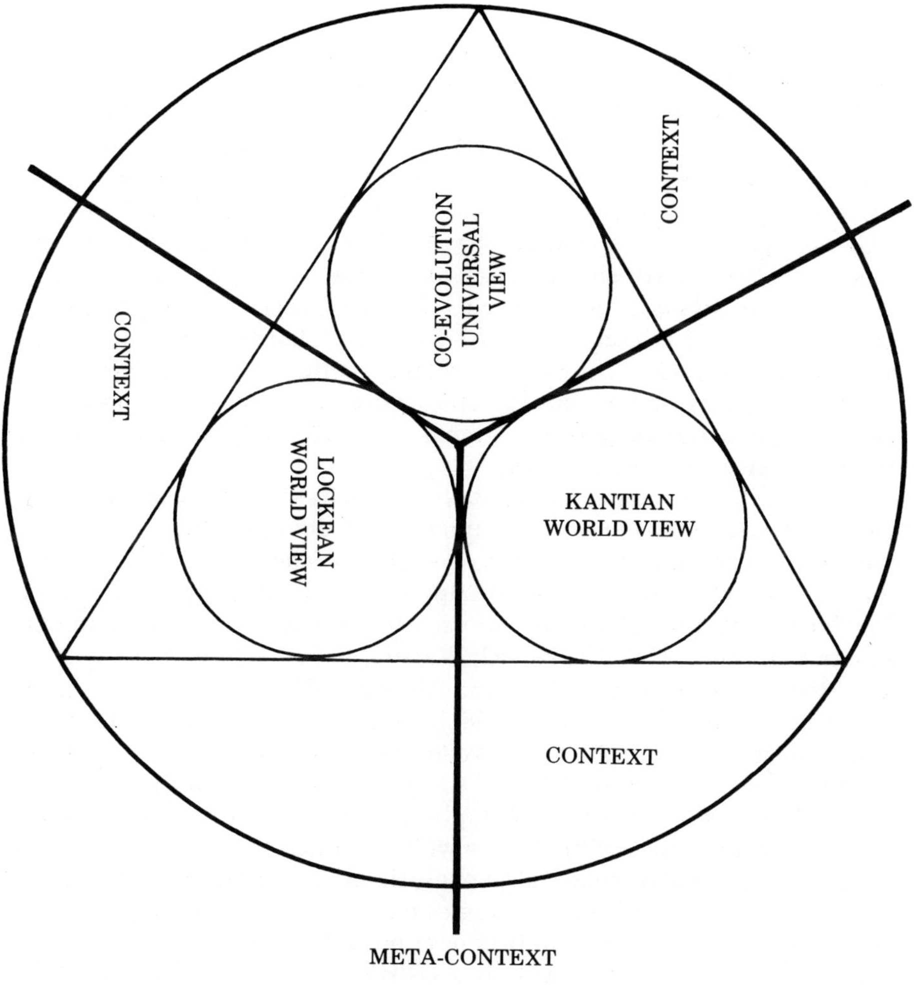

Father: . . . I am not asking another question. . . . I am making the same question bigger. Every time we add a related piece to the question, we get more clues to what sort of answer we should expect.
Daughter: So now we have six pieces of the question?
Father: . . . All your six make up together a triangular sort of question and that triangle is to be related to what's in this book. [p. 213]

He hinted that the pattern that connects sincere questioning process concerning *Mind and Nature* (1979) involves something sacred. That is, clues may be found in some "ECO" (logical) complexity of greater geometric progression (Spherical Triangular). ECO is the "incorruptible and therefore not mocked" ecological god of "the search for eternal verities that characterize the world" (Bateson and Bateson, 1987, pp. 142–143) and involves change of view. For example, a spherical triangle involves a pattern comprised of a plane passing through its center, which overlays a "great circle." Figure 7 (page 57) re-presents a "basic secret" of trigonometry (Radius and Chord). Taken from the science of geometrics, The Legend, though technical, seem surprisingly fitting involving meta-context. The figure involves linear, circular, recursive, and triadic patterns—lending the extra dimension of depth to larger patterns that connect.

Ultimately, the secret of life itself, found as giving molecular structure to DNA, is based on a 3-dimensional double-helical model. Its pattern of rigid *complementary* paired bases—adenine to thymine and guanine to cytosine is bound in triplicate by hydrogen. Its discovery involved re-cognizing the key *connecting pattern* of a double-diamond image at its core (Nobel Prize '62; Watson, Crick Wilkins).

Remember, however, the romantic eternal triangles of times past. As so, there remains the compulsion to mediate (behavioral, Lockean assumption) reconciliation between recursive patterns of battling members of negative coalitions, i.e., Locke and Kant. Catherine Bateson (1985) cited the need for metaphorical patterns of organization for "increasing our stock of models as well as changing or abandoning old ones" (p. 45). From a universal co-evolutional paradigm she constructed and patterned the triadic new metaphor of responsibly "co-parenting the earth" to replace the well-known outdated caption picturing our planet from outer space: "YOUR MOTHER, LOVE HER OR LEAVE HER!" Bateson's new organizational metaphor evolved from families inventing alternative structures. She held "how we live in the world should be based on the concept of co-parenthood, that together we give birth to and foster the future" (p. 45). This therapeutic triadic metaphor of co-parenting the earth transfers well from what was once called "a civilized divorce" to the universal implications of the pattern of a symmetrically escalating international nuclear arms race. Catherine Bateson (1985) described and patterned how

> We are locked in a relationship with the Russians from which we cannot entirely extricate ourselves. For many reasons, we do not like them and we don't trust them, and there is no love lost. But the test is to try and handle the negotiation of daily, monthly, yearly relations without escalating into conflict . . . for the sake of the children, for the sake of the planet . . . working together for the sake of the future *is* possible—even when love is dead even when there has been mutual pain and insult. [p. 45]

Bateson's (1985) metaphor of co-parenting the earth, she held, "transfers well," reflecting a change of patterned attitude from organized competition escalating to conflict and *revolutions* (destructive triangulation of the planet) toward an attitude of cooperation and ethical tolerance of humanity, the world, and our universe (therapeutic triangulation). Bowen's (cited in Guerin, 1976, p. 76) conceptual pattern of detriangulation of previously rigid pathological triangles theoretically fits Bateson's metaphor patterned as of co-parenting the earth; that is, it is inferred that the interactional meta pattern of organization of Identified Patient (IP) has been the pathological future of our planet: the United States and the USSR symbolize a symmetrical battling coalition.

This section of the pattern of the literature review goes *beyond,* without the possibility of ever leaving behind, patterns of a cybernetic epistemology. Accordingly, the following involves Jantsch's (1980) "emerging paradigm of 'meta'-evolution," more of von Foerster's (Segal, 1986) radical constructivism, and Maturana's theory of structure determinism—as von Foerster held Segal (1986) invented. Together they emerge to make up a radical patterned *Third Wave* (Toffler, 1980) of second order cybernetics—based on subjective or self-referential processes, complexity and autonomy—"the highest [non-hierarchical] order of recursion" (Keeney, 1983, p. 99): the *fractal* (meaning it reveals new complexity on smaller and smaller scales) bespeaks Jantsch's (1980) complex account of "metaevolutionary processes" (pp. 218–226).

Jantsch's (1980) "new paradigm of self-organization" is aimed at a new synthesis of an up-to-date "'ecoystem' of new scientific concepts . . . not older than a decade . . . ; [of which one] most fascinating

"*Equilateral Geodetic Triangulation:* Process of triangulation where the curvature of the area is great or where obstructions between points require structures built, so that one point may be seen from another, so that the whole area can be mapped. Two points, miles apart, are selected, the line between is measured as the base line. The third point is determined by the angle it makes with each end of the base line . . . Geodetic triangulation is the theory and practice of determining the position of points in the earths surface and the dimensions of areas so large that the curvature of the earth must be taken into account" *(Columbia Encyclopedia,* 2d Ed. [1950], p. 761).

"*PLANE TRIGONOMETRY: Radius & Chord.* The primitive but enduring fact that there is a constant relationship between the diameter of any circle—expressed as the circumference [which is] three times the diameter . . . the ratio is 3 . . . it can never be calculated exactly . . . this [is an] unvarying relationship, plus the fact that the radius equals ½ the diameter, follows also a relationship between a central angle, the radius the circle lies in, and the chord . . . If that chord be cut in half and a line be drawn from the vertex of the angle to its mid-point, we will have a right triangle. . . . The parent double triangle, all the elements of this right triangle are tied in to the constant relationship of the radius and the circumference. We can draw a bigger circle . . . in which the length of the sides would change. But the angle at the center would stay the same; so too would the ratio of the sides to each other . . . they would be corresponding sides of a triangle similar to the first one in the smaller circle. . . . Solutions may be arrived at by considering adjoining triangles *(Encyclopedia Americana,* 1961 vol. 27 pp. 59–62).

Figure 7. Transient Therapeutic Triangulation

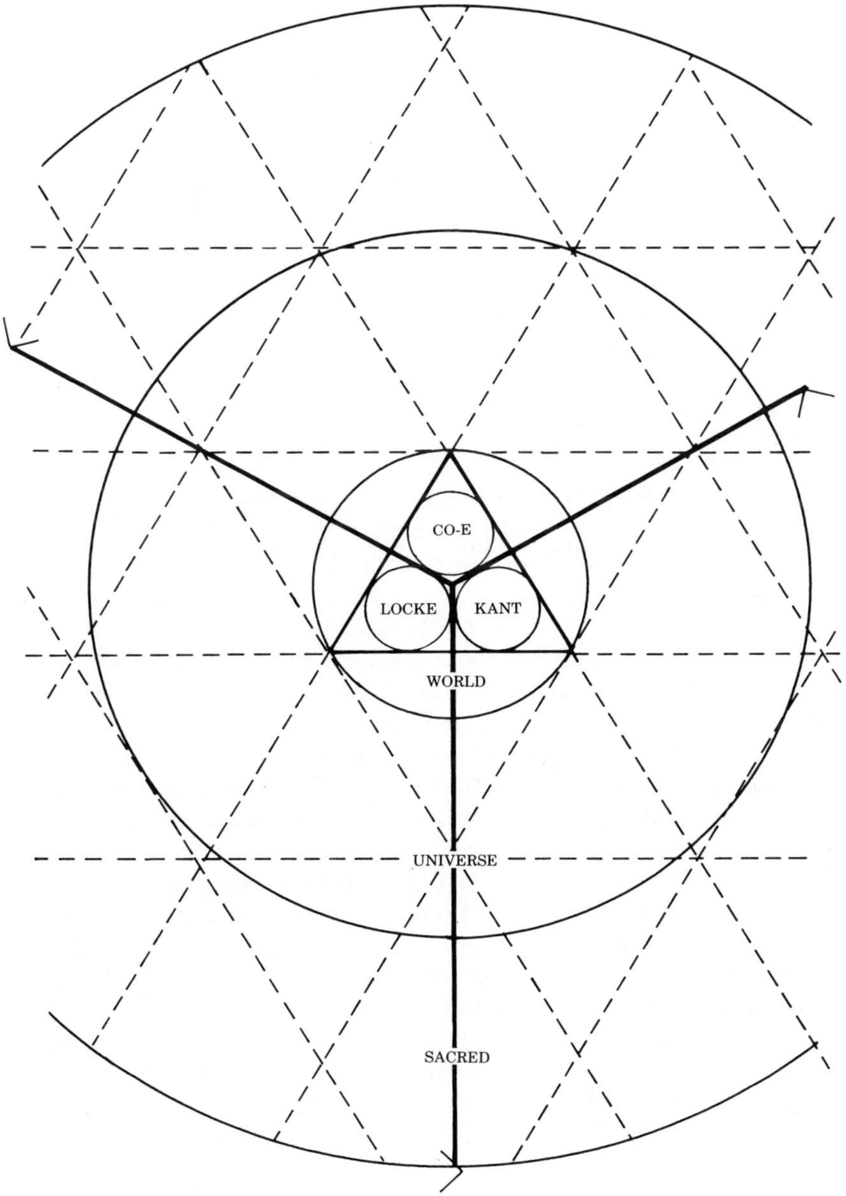

aspect . . . is the dynamics with which they [concepts] seem to organize themselves into the more comprehensive paradigm—which thereby furnishes its own proof" (p.xiii). Complex patterns of a self-organizing paradigm of co-evolution act as catalyst for the involvement of Nobel laureate Prigone's theory of "dissipative structures" (1967), which allows "self-transcendence." A dissipative structure is understood as chemically volatile arranged patterns of "a material structure organizing the flow of matter . . . both descriptions are equally valid. They constitute two sides of *complementarity.*" At a meta-level of self-organization, patterns reveal "energy systems manifest themselves in the organization of material processes and structures" (p. 35). Jantsch (1980), a master cybernetician, went well beyond any generalized pattern of description of a cybernetic epistemology thus far. The aesthetic complexity of his descriptive patterns of co-evolution as self-organizing illustrates "On *Being* Cybernetic Epistemologists." Jantsch's (1980) theory held:

> The central aspects of the emerging paradigm of self-organization are: *primo,* a specific macroscopic dynamics of process systems; *secundo,* continuous exchange and thereby co-evolution with the environment, and *tertio,* self-transcendence, the evolution of evolutionary processes.
>
> [p. 9]

This emergent paradigm organizing co-evolution is profoundly humanistic; with self-transcendence ("meta-evolution") there is a "reaching out beyond the boundaries of one's own existence, the joy of creation." Jantsch's (1980) broad theme gives scientific foundation to the "all embracing phenomonon of evolution," not, he is quick to add, the stereotyped (Darwinian) theory of survival of the species as a "game in which the only reward is to stay in the game," or one of patterned "heroic pessimism" that posits "the only origin of life as an accidental once-in-a-lifetime event" (p. xiii). Co-evolution pictures it is organized along *"a non-dualistic perspective,"* thereby intuitively fulfilling the latent "wish" for a new paradigm that transcends patterns of organization of linearity, circularity, pendulum shifts, and recursive battling dyads. There is a "new ordering principle," according to Jantsch, patterned as gaining "order through fluctuation" which has to do with patterns of "action and heat" (thermodynamic perturbations) in volatile chemical reactions involving Prigone's (1967) theoretical dissipative structures.

Jantsch's (1980) complex "unifying paradigm of self-organization" comprehensively exposes the co-evolutionary path of a sample of "far from equilibrium dissipative structures," which he defined as being contemporary scientists/scholars (Bateson, Maturana, Ilya Prigone, Varela, von Foerster, et al.) creatively sharing and synthesizing a "*new world view* which emphasizes (paradoxically dualistically) process over structure, nonequilibrium over equilibrium, evolution over permanence, and individual creativity over collective stabilization." Jantsch held that "from an understanding of non-*dualistic,* creative sharing in evolution arises a new sense of meaning" (1980, back cover). His conceptualization fits Hoffman's (1981) prescriptive edicts for "The 'Second Generation' new epistemology, based on an evolutionary paradigm" (pp. 344–349).

Meaning arises in patterns beyond self-transcendence and beyond reflexive schismogenic double-bind Games Without End; beyond the pattern of dizzying Revolutionary cul-de-sac; beyond the recursive dance patterns of polar shifts of seventeenth-century world views, and, most importantly, involves awareness of the *dangerous* patterned metastability of *revolutionary shifts* of Kuhn's paradigm theory. For the complex meta-patterns of fractalization of self-organization portrayed co-evolution as occurring historically/scientifically through breaks in escalating *symmetry!* Jantsch's (1980) chapter "Evolution—Revolution"

> points to a profound dilemma in which the human world finds itself thanks to order through fluctuations . . . the *metastability* of political, social and economic structures is enhanced. But this also means an *increasing danger* that the fluctuations get bigger and bigger and may become disastrous . . . [witness] the arsenal of nuclear weapons.
>
> [italics added] [p. 17]

"Runaway" patterns or "escalating symmetrical escalations" spell chaos leading to catastrophe—breaks in *symmetry* are recorded by Jantsch, though, as *meta-evolutionary,* not *revolutionary.* Furthermore, Jantsch's (1980) use of the theory of dissipative structures shares a "fundamental homology" or pattern of true relatedness mode, which "makes it possible to view . . . phenomenon dynamically linking many *levels!* (p. 11.)

Central to Jantsch's (1980) universal view is the thesis of self-organizing patterns of "connectedness" and "symmetry breaks," which transcend and heal the "dualistic split between nature and culture . . . " "We are evolution" (p. 8) is his construct. Jantsch agreed with Bateson's (1979) conceptual metaphor of the pattern in processes of a "self-healing tautology"

> the world of mental process, is both tautological and ecological . . . [a] slowly self-healing tautology. Left to itself, any large piece . . . will tend

to settle toward tautology, that is toward *internal consistency* of ideas and processes . . . every now and then, the consistency gets torn; breaks up like the surface of a pond when a stone is thrown into it. Then the tautology slowly but immediately starts to heal . . . the healing may be ruthless. Whole species may be exterminated in the process.

[italics added] [p. 206]

Cybernetic epistemologists recognize patterns and organization. According to Festinger's (1957) theory of cognitive dissonance, the larger universal view of Jantsch (1980) is *consonant* or fits patterns of organized psychological "logic." On the other hand, is Jantsch's (1980) meta-complex aesthetic pattern of a self-organizing universe a new "process of knowing maintaining and constructing a new world of experience," an ambitious potent exercise in *inventing* reality? Are the patterns and organization of the models presented in this study real or invented? Resoundingly, "YES! Both/and" would be the answer of radical constructivists!

Segal (1986) depicted von Foerster's radical constructivism as *The Dream of Reality*. Segal succinctly addressed the intuitive, lingering wish for a new paradigm this way:

1) we wish reality to *exist independently* of us, we who observe it.
2) we wish reality to be *discoverable,* to reveal itself to us. We wish to know its secrets, i.e., how it works.
3) we wish these secrets to be *lawful,* so we can predict and ultimately control reality.
4) we wish for *certainty;* we wish to know that what we discovered about reality is true.

[p. 3]

The common denominator of these four wishes is the singular pattern of demonstrative *objectivity*. This, Segal (1986) related, is the price of the constructivist's world view; "one must replace the notion of objectivity with that of responsibility" (p. 4). "Radical constructivism" has taken on "the unpopular job of shattering the fantasy of objective reality." Constructivists claim "there are no data, no laws of nature, no external objects—independent of observers" (p. 3). Hence the epistolary is that constructivists "embrace self-reference and recursion" (p. 43):

Constructivism identifies . . . through the lens of epistemology, the limits of what we can know. The primary aim . . . is not to find fault with traditional epistemologies, but to account for the basis of cognition. The totality of our mental faculties, without first assuming an independent reality. Constructivists argue that to understand the world we must begin by understanding ourselves, i.e., the observers.

[Segal, 1986, p. 4]

Moreover, in a mini-review of the literature on constructivism, Efram and Lukens (1986) recounted: "What the constructivists are saying about us these days." Traditionally, they refer to "the so-called 'cognitive revolution,'" according to triage priority Bruner, Gazzaniga, and Watzlawick. They relate how each author employs a different "level of analysis" involving cognitive processes—reminding us "how little we know about ourselves and each other" (p. 65). The common theme of constructivists, according to the authors, is "the centrality of the human process of constructing, exchanging and believing in narratives . . . we create products of mind . . . the epistemological stance that we *create* through our transactions, the world we think we see" (p. 66); that is, verbal patterns of thought create our world view.

A Varela chapter, included in Watzlawick's (1984) *The Invented Reality,* portrays the impossibility of matching interpretations of the world that are objective and absolute:

whenever we do try and find the source of say a perception or an idea, we find ourselves in an ever-receding *fractal* [sic], and wherever we choose to delve we find it equally full of details and interdependencies. It is always the perception of a perception of a perception. . . . Or the description of a description of a description. . . . There is nowhere we can drop anchor and say, this is where this perception started: this is how it was done.

[italics added]
[cited in Efram and Lukens, 1986, p. 67]

In the foregoing concise account of constructivists books, Efram and Lukens (1986) quoted how Bruner laments that we are emerging from a "dark passage" of history and have, he hopes, learned that "man is not an island, entire of itself, but a part of the culture he inherits and then re-constructs" (p. 68). The review concluded with the author's shared response to a constructivist's philosophy: "The moment we delve a bit into the process through which meanings are acquired and promulgated . . . our arrogance dissipates . . . replaced by healthy tentativeness concerning our systems of belief" (pp. 65–68).

Segal (1986) summarized the primary claim of radical constructivism: "We CONSTRUCT or INVENT reality," as opposed to discovering it. First "we fool ourselves" by dividing it in two realities. *Reality one* is the "subjective world" of our experience. *Reality two* is the "so-called objective world of Reality." Understanding is predicated on the perceived consonance/dissonance/irrelevance in the "match game" of a patterned world that exists "out there" and our experiential world (p. 17). Reality two significantly matches the patterns of Bateson's (1972) Learning II; reality one matches those patterns of Learning Level III.

Consequently, von Foerster (cited in Segal, 1986) addressed two examples of this "un-pattern" constructivist change in thinking: (1) According to Einstein's theory of relativity, "observations are not absolute but relative to the point of view, " as in the "match game" above, a coordinate system (p. 29). (2) Next, according to Heisenberg's uncertainty principle, "observations affect the observed so as to obliterate the observer's hope of predictions" uncertainty is absolute (p. 30); that is, unpredictable patterns emerge.

Segal's (1986) representation of von Foerster's constructivism devotes an entire chapter to the neurophilosoper Maturana, who advocates defining observer-based science by explicitly defining statements as integrative or subjective-dependent, "uniting the observer and his observations" (p. 60). Maturana claimed that there are "four classes of operations that must be coherent to validate a scientific explanation"; he called these:

[OPERATIONS OF DISTINCTION]

1) *Make a distinction:* . . . write a recipe specifying what actions an observer must perform to perceive a phenomenon.
2) *Construct an explanatory hypothesis:* . . . if the explanatory system is left to operate, it will generate the phenomenon to explain.
3) *Compute:* . . . another phenomenon the system in step 2 will generate if left to operate.
4) *Validate:* . . . engage in operations . . . observe the phenomenon computed in #3. If phenomenon can be observed the explanation in step #2 is validated. The experimental system is isomorphic to the phenomenon.

[p. 60—61]

For example, normally if a scientist is asked if unicorns exist, he will say, "No." Objectively, only certain animals exist in reality. Maturana first asked what *operations of distiction* are needed to observe a unicorn. If one needs to go to a museum, Maturana says, "Yes, at a museum unicorns exist." One must specify the operations to satisfy colleagues. "Speaking in this way makes clear that a unicorn needs an observer to come into being" (cited in Segal, 1986, p. 62); that is, one must distinguish *how* reality is constructed to validate scientific explanations.

Relatedly, Maturana stated "The problem—is how to talk." Indeed: "Everything that is said is said by an observer to another observer who may be him or herself" (p. 60). It might be said that the human organism constructs a phenomenal view of the world, others, and self. That is, s/he organizes patterns by nominalizing, prioritizing, categorizing, computing, and correlating cognitions. This is done in what the author calls seemingly disorganized chaotic patterns of thinking-language (th-lang), in a non-stop inner-dialogue of thought-talk (th-alk), which cognitivists call self-talk. In agreement, Segal (1986) thus examines

> *the relationship between language, thinking and our view of reality. Language operating below our level of everyday consciousness, structures our thinking by punctuating circular streams of interaction into one-way causalities. It nominalizes processes and unwittingly seduces us into habitual causal schemes for explaining the world.*
>
> [*pp. 58–59*]

The problem might not be how to talk, but rather the nature of patterns that organize "th-lang" used by humans "th-alking," as busily re-constructing and inventing views of the self, others, and the universe.

With Maturana an objective universe is replaced by a patterned "multiverse, where many observer 'verses' co-exist, each valid in its own right" (Efram and Lukens, 1985, p. 25). His theory is that "living systems are 'structure determined' and 'informationally closed'" organisms. They survive by "structure coupling"—in pattern fit with one another and the surrounding medium ("soup"). Organisms are involved in a pattern of "purposeless drift" of continual patterns of drift of external and internal perturbations until their time of death—which is immanent but uncertain and unpredictable as to time and place. Organisms are also seen as observing systems who describe, distinguish, and delineate in patterns of words and symbols called language and, as so, hold that without the observer nothing exists. "As structure determined organisms we do not perceive an objective universe—the objects we think we see are a product of the nervous system" (p. 24). Maturana's construct (cited in Dell, 1985) insists, "We are in the world like hanging from a string immersing ourselves in various soups and describing the world by our change of state according to the particular soup in which we are immersed" (p. 17). The patterns organizing COGNITION are all!

Relatedly, Paul Dell (1985, pp. 1–20) continued to ponder Maturana's theory of structure determinism, coupling it in pattern to Bateson's epistemology and bestowing "biological ontology" to structure determinism as "a foundation for social and behavioral sciences" (p.

1). Two interesting points he considered are: (1) The pattern of "structure coupling"—constructed as the phenomenon underlying and constituting cognition or intelligence. To be structure coupled is to behave aesthetically, as one is patterned to, with intelligence with other organisms and the environment. In other words, Maturana theoretically couples with the Kantian assumption of a pro forma (a priori) intellect. In addition, according to cognitive theory one behaves intelligently by keeping one's patterned "intellect" over emotions, i.e., $\frac{\text{intellect}}{\text{emotion}}$. (2) Second (Dell ponders), the concept of "informationally closed"—theoretically information does not exist, as with pro forma intellect the pattern of " 'informations' " all there before birth, or "what you 'get' is what you 'see.' " Any change is determined by the patterned organizational structure of the organism, i .e., the Kantian categories. In other words, "Toasters—Toast!" (Becvar, R., 1985). Consequently, change occurs through perturbations and thermal fluctuations of prepatterned cognitions. An analogy-like Greek parody may help clear up rising questions. Using Maturana's "soup" metaphor and relating it to the pattern of reciprocal structure coupling of learning/teaching. Students and teachers are informationally closed organisms: Picture each suspended by separate strings immersed in the same kettle of stew (the medium). To some the stew is too cold; to others it is too hot; to a few it is just right for structure coupling! The pattern of reciprocal process popularly known as teaching/learning is in theory structure coupling—both student and teacher indulge in seemingly erratic patterns of perturbation of themselves and each other—mostly through the *medium* of patterned language exchanged and the aforementioned th-alk and th-lang (self-talk). Now the medium is made up of the patterned organizational language and paradigms of the particular scientific community the kettle holds. The thermal fluctuations, i.e., too cold, hot, or just right, affect and are affected by the organisms immersed. (One hesitates to extend this construct to outside the kettle of learning/teaching—other kettles could be home, work, church, et cetera.) The "vegetables and meat" in this particular stew could be nearly "raw, mushy, of falling apart"—involving irratic thermal/perturbation dynamics—these ingredients might be (paradigms) made up from fresh, frozen, refrigerated, or left-over from an indeterminable time. The point is that they contribute to the pattern of consistency of the medium and how free or restrained the patterns organizing each structure determined organisms are to couple. Each is free or restrained only by its patterned organized structure determinism, to couple with the patterns of medium alone, with others, or both—all that *might* be required *is* and to behave with patterned

$\frac{\text{intelligence}}{\text{emotions}}$ when perturbed or perturbing about *patterns of organization* in the medium. Structure determined organisms, involved in structure coupling, while cognizant of their patterns of keeping $\frac{\text{intellect}}{\text{emotion}}$ probably agree that "this [organizational] stew is better than any Mom ever made!"

Having gone dangerously beyond the patterns of becoming a cybernetic epistemologist, it is fitting that the emerging patterns of the "unifying paradigm of self-organization" (Jantach, 1981), radical constructivism, and structure determinism are seen to structure couple with von Foerster's constructivist's edicts (cited in Segal, 1986):

> ETHICAL IMPERATIVE: Act always so as to increase the number of choices . . .
>
> MORAL IMPERATIVE: A is better off when B is better off . . . For constructivists, life is a non-zero sum game: all players win or all players lose. Cooperation not competition is the sine qua non of social existence . . . and replacing the notion of objectivity with that of responsibility. [p. 4]

Although in the end, Rosenthal (1984), like Maturana and von Foerster, specified, in *Words and Values,* that it is organizational patterns of:

> language [which] can show us interconnections and reciprocal interactions and mutual inter-dependencies, but it can't tell us what to do once we've seen them . . . it can't help us decide which to consider more important . . . It can lead us to see everything as a system comprised of interrelated parts; to see the world as an integrated whole . . . it can take us that far. But it can't tell us what—if we really could get the whole world in our hands—what we should do with it. . . .
>
> [p. 250]

And so, in the Emergent and Beyond patterned hypothetical therapeutic triangulation of the new (co-evolutionary) universal view, one feels nurtured by the warm fuzziness of the aesthetics involved, for according to Jantsch (1980): "In the domain of self-organizing systems, information is also capable of organizing itself; new knowledge arises" (p. 11). The author views Jantsch's epistolary of a self-organizing universe as a meta-cybernetic pattern, that is in its pattern of non-hierarchical involvement and inclusion of other patterned views (linear, circular, simple cybernetic and cybernetics of cybernetics or second order cybernetics).

Immanently, however, indications are that geometric analog computer graphic patterns are creating "New images of chaos that are stirring a science *revolution*" (Gleick, 1987, pp. 122-134). Gleick wrote of late seventies, physics graduate faculty—made up of youthful, innovative, responsible mentor/professors—and resourceful, structured graduate programs, which were thought to be a good match for the onslaught of an information explosion involving an expected incoming "student body of bright nonconformists." It came about, though, that what these mature graduate students "wanted to learn, no one could teach." They represented a "special breed of researchers [who], armed with complex equations and computer graphics, saw *patterns* where others saw only disorder." Soon, the physics "department found itself confronted by a tiny *revolution,* an uprising among [its] graduate students" (p. 122); Economically unfunded and with mentor forewarning, just ten years later, these "fledgling" scientists of complex pattern to chaos have "begun to change decision processes . . . " in micro to macro-systems of business, economics, astronomy and in "the way political theorists talk about the stresses leading to armed *conflict*" (p. 123). Today physiologists "believe that chaos provides a way of predicting and perhaps treating . . . erratic rhythms in the process that govern life, from breathing to heartbeats to brain function" (p. 134).

Gleick's (1987) account of researchers who had cut their teeth on "*traditional education* concentrated on systems that were *linear* . . . [that] obey laws of proportionality . . . [but intuited and found] most real-world systems are *nonlinear*" (p. 127). They began in a "no-name" field by "plugging and unplugging . . . building up various combinations of circuitry . . . " (p. 124) using various factors and an analog computer; they linked *cords of emergent theory* of random and chaos. They *coupled* two point "strange attractors" (meteorology), *fractal geometry* (mathematical—family of patterns), inventing linkages between seemingly unrelated "whole families of chaotic systems," theory that linked "turbulent fluids to fluctuating electric circuits to the rhythms of life itself" (p. 123).

Working backward, the "game they would play" involved *triadic equations* and unknown patterns of strange attractors. Visual patterns ruled: "you don't see something until you have the *right metaphor* to let you perceive it" (p. 128). Attractors ran from "ordinary to strange: first, steady states (where everything stops); then periodic cycles (where everything oscillates: then chaotic strange attractors (everything else)" (p. 132). "For a periodically cyclical system like the pendulum clock the diagram would be a *loop*" (p. 124) (suggestive of complementary/symmetrical recursion). An action photograph "represented a cyclical system fluctuating around two points" (p. 126), its image strikingly similar to the one used in this study's geometric descriptions of recursion—the lazy-eight pattern of Becvar and Becvar (1982, p. 7; p. 29) (figures 4 and 5). A magnetic pendulum, a "system of three equations . . . " computer analoged how a "chaotic system never repeats itself in a periodic way, . . . [it] never looped around on itself in the same way. . . . It formed an intricate, *recursive* shape, a sort of double spiral, curling first one way and then the next. . . . It seemed to have a *life of its own*" (p. 126).

In experimental interval graphing of analog patterns "often . . . *three* dimensions were necessary to see the structure, . . . no problem. Instead of plotting each interval against the next, . . . [they] would plot each interval against each of the next two. It was a *trick*—a gimmick. . . . [a] *three-dimensional* graph required knowledge of *three* independent variables in a system. The trick gave *three* variables for the price of one. . . . In *three* dimensions, especially the *patterns emerged. . . .* " Matching experimental data to analog computer-generated data revealed that "the real data was always fuzzier, smeared out by noise. Yet [in the computer model] the structure was unmistakable" (p. 132). Reversing the trend toward reductionism, the new science of the structure of chaos, and organizational patterns of . . . is "more interested in the idea of the whole can be greater than the sum of the parts" [italics added throughout] (p. 134). Gleick's *Chaos: Making a New Science* (1987) chronicles this new non-conformist science that involves "nonlinear twists" to looking back, between and beyond the lines (gaps and loopholes) of apparant disorder, to random and chaos, evolving new three-dimensional patterns that connect—change of world view.

Chapter 4 presents the Research Approach; the heuristic approach provided an appropriate research frame for inquiry involving the chaos of Bateson's (1972, 1979, 1987) Learning Level III or cybernetic epistemology.

CHAPTER 3

Heuristic Approach to Research—"What Is As It Is . . ."

Introductory Remarks—Literature Review

Gowin (Thomas, Ed., 1972), in his chapter, "Methodological Questions," in the *1972 NSSE Yearbook on Philosophical Redirection of Educational Research,* described criteria consonant with this study:

> The educative process is almost always a process of, from . . . to., . . . the process is developmental, episodic, continuous . . . the person begins in some state . . . and moves through the process in a variety of ways toward some ending point of maturity, skill, knowledge, changed belief. . . . Studies in logic or epistemology . . . may be valid in themselves, but, unless a special study is made bringing findings over into the educational context, nothing follows for educational practice.
>
> [p. 15]

The traditional/residual conceptual frames of the study relate to patterns of educative process. Popkewitz (1984) pursued the importance of a pattern of paradigm elements forming unarticulated second order "rules of the game" that underlie and give direction to scientific work as well. The patterned elements of research suggest that science has

> emotional and political as well as cognitive elements. As people are trained in a research community, they learn ways to think, 'see,' 'feel,' and act toward the world. The dispositions . . . are implicit in the exemplars of a field that the researcher learns as s/he defines the scope and boundary of inquiry.
>
> [p. 33]

Popkewitz went on to view the pattern of underlying assumptions of a paradigm as having "different layers of abstraction . . . exist[ing] simultaneously and superimposed upon one another" (p. 33). In other words, Popkewitz might view the preceding patterned models as comprising a heuristic mosaic of sorts. In agreement, Broudy in the *NSSE Yearbook* cited that laws that govern structure of parts "are not sufficient to describe the principles of their integration. . . . The theory of emergents [states] that properties not contained in their constituents" (Thomas, Ed., 1972, p. 230) *emerge*—i.e. "the whole is greater than the sum of its parts, or 1 + 1 = 3" (Becvar and Becvar, 1982, p. 24).

Still in a residual frame, Patton (1980), prefacing a quotation of Kuhn's paradigm theory, described how

> the more insidious type of theoretical disposition is the global or macro-level theory that constitutes a basic paradigm organizing the researcher's view . . . researchers have been throughly socialized into a particular paradigmatic view . . . no longer aware that their perception has been shaped by theoretical blinders.
>
> [p. 277]

According to the quotation by Kuhn (1962, 1970) (cited in Patton, 1980) the researcher's world view is patterned as "second-nature." The work of scientists progresses through educationally acquired models, i.e., paradigms—"more binding and complete than any set of rules for research . . . abstracted from them" (p. 46).

Paradoxically, research focus is summed up by Douglas (1976) as "a basic predisposition to hold *either* a consensus *or* conflict view of society," the "self, others, and the world" (Ellis, 1975). Accordingly, scientists approach their research "problem" from differing patterned predispositions which should be made explicit" (Douglas, 1976, p. 277). At this point, Patton (1980) offered a paradoxical "paradigm of choice" *either* the "Classical (cooperative) Paradigm of Society" *or* the "Conflict Paradigm of Society." (See paradoxical either/or meta–double-bind, chapter 2, pp. 22–23.)

The dualistic organized pattern of the "paradigm of choice" Patton (1980) proposed has recently been brought to question by Auger (1987), who held with Maturana's (1975, 1978) theory of structure determinism; Auger (1987) professed having come to the organized "conclusion that human beings are more or less completely 'choice' determined. . . . Others have maintained that humans are free . . . they are not determined" (p. 49). In other words, Auger questions if one can ultimately "choose" or change his/her mind, in light of epistemological patterns of assumptions and Maturana's theory.

The continuing patterned dilemma was cited by Homan (1967) and quoted by Popkewitz (1984) in his book on research methodology:

> If [the conditions of social science being historically influenced] make trouble for us as social scientists, remember that they are a great advantage to humanity, by leaving men the *illusion of choice.* I speak of the illusion because I myself believe that what each of us does is absolutely determined.
>
> [p. 1]

It may well be that nowhere else in this study/inquiry was the patterned phenomenon of paradigm shift reflected more vividly or the dissonance more profound than in the *choice* of research paradigm. For according to Kuhn (1962, 1970), it is assumed that "scientists know [key patterns of] what the world is like" (p. 5), how its patterns are organized and structured.

Many distinguished academic writers preserve the old patterns of organized solutions that maintained past problems in education. For example, Bloom (1987) in his provocative best-selling critique of higher education *The Closing of the American Mind,* argues rhetorically that *closed-minded* higher education has "flunked" students of democracy. Paradoxically, open-minded higher education is targeted as having precipitated summa summarum (the sum total) of political and social crises of America and "impoverished souls of today's students." Conversion, according to Bloom, lies with "higher education," teaching its graduate students born-again democratic ideals, which should, in turn, "unpollute" educational/intellectual "failures," thereby restoring America's socio/policital/institutional rigor and health. Reviewers have likened this (anti-feminist/anti-liberation) work as having the dis-organizing "force and effect" of "what electric-shock therapy must be like. . . . "It's like 'My God, our whole language, our *whole view of the world* has changed and . . . it's somehow German [Kantian patterned] in origin,' " (1987, June 3, *St. Louis Post Dispatch,* "You," pp. 1 9). In a fashion similar to Jantsch's (1980) pattern of description of a return to "religio" or Ferguson's (1980) critique of "back to basic simple solutions," Bellow in the introduction to *The Closing of the American Mind* prescribed a much repeated historical pattern of a return to the old philosophers, i.e., Plato, Socrates, Aristotle, to sniff-out and "detect the untreated sewage odors of the [last] century of *revolutionary* rhetoric" (p. 17). Bellow described how the university has become "inundated and saturated with the backflow of society's 'problems' " (p. 18). Paradoxically, Bloom posited "openness and value relativism" and the "demos" (common people) as the demons to be exorcised by a patterned organized *shift* to golden age philosophical politics in education. It seems that the pattern of conflict theory dates back at least two millennia to Socrates's scholarly (and lethal) triumph of "Man's" reason over "the laws of nature and [matricentric] gods rule." Bloom (1987), however, seemed to prefer the pattern of an Americanization of Locke's world view—as opposed to the view of Kant. He held: "However, the unity of the university is now Kant" (p. 300). To this Bloom (1987) added: "The old tragic conflicts reappear newly labeled . . . *Choice* is all the rage these days . . . modern philosophy is moving toward no-fault insurance, no-fault divorce, and no-fault choices" (p. 228). As for the truth and value of the pattern of organized scientific endeavors: "One sees a bit of decay around the edges of its good conscience, formerly so robust. Books like Thomas Kuhn's *The Structure of Scientific Revolutions* are popular symptoms of this condition" [p. 200]. Patterns of organization of resolution of the paradox of either/or choice of research paradigms lies in meta-heuristic approaches according to Douglass and Moustakas (1985), pp. 35–55).

Heuristic Inquiry

An approach outlined by Douglass and Moustakas (1985) as "Heuristic Inquiry: The Internal Search to Know" (pp. 39–55) fits the process and praxis involved in a meta-search that encourages the researcher and guides the process of asking the first questions about a theme of inquiry. The theme of this study/inquiry is: "change of world view," which involves the patterned phenomena of cognitive dissonance (Festinger, 1957) at Bateson's (1972) Level II Learning and what the author calls "cybernetic shock" of Bateson's (1972) Level III Learning changes (pp. 287–306).

Douglass and Moustakas (1985, pp. 39–55) described this framework as "offering a disciplined pursuit of essential meanings connected with . . . significant human experience" (p. 39), that of labyrinth paths to becoming a cybernetic epistemologist. The heuristic attitude required "a passionate and personal involvement at problem solving [Learning II] and an effort to know the essence of some aspect of life through the internal pathways of the self" (p. 39). Exploration of connecting meta-patterns are involved at Bateson's Learning Level of change III.

The word *heuristic* comes from the Greek meaning: "I find," related to scientists'/scholars' descriptively familiar "eureka" or "aha" experience. Accordingly, heuristic inquiry requires a Learning III subjective process "that affirms imagination, intuition, self-reflection and the tacit dimension as valid . . . in the search for knowledge and understanding" (p. 40) of the patterns of change of world view. The rationale for considering the heuristic approach involved the experience of patterned dissonance of paradoxical either/or thinking and the "shock" of complexity of cybernetic both/and thinking—and beyond. The pattern leads to the path to Being, as "becoming a cybernetic epistemologist—and *knowing* it." The pattern of experiential process (Learning II and III) involved the researcher as a complete participant observer in the residual patterned phenomenon of "Revolutions as Change of World View" (Kuhn, 1962, 1970, pp. 111–35). Graduate students' patterns of learning experience of cybernetic epistemology (L. III), described in the review of the literature, may be reflected as patterned dissonance (L. II) and in the depth and duration of *cybernetic shock* (L. III) manifest in one's self and peers. According to Douglass and Moustakas (1985), the researcher is heuristically awakened and inspired by the pattern of processes of "reflecting, exploring, sifting and elucidating the nature of the phenomenon" (p. 40) under study/inquiry. Ultimately, heuristic inquiry's purpose is to illuminate the theme and generate a pattern of focused questions.

The patterned process of the heuristic approach is generally consonant with qualitative methodology. The first vital step was the passionate disciplined commitment of the researcher in drawing the distinct theme: change of world view; then followed the researcher's punctuation of the pattern of questions for study from the review of the literature. The pattern of research study questions was: (1) *Who* conceived the framework for world views? (2) *What* do meta-assumptions have to do with change of world view? (3) *When* does world view change? (4) *Where* does acquisition of world view begin? (5) *Why* does one change world view? (6) *How* does world view change?

Generally, literature review answers evolved from the researcher's punctuation of a pattern for organizing study, that of *traditional, residual,* and *emergent/beyond* concepts of change of world view. With distinct theme and focused questions the researcher experienced the pattern of dissonant drive involved with the traditional/residual paradoxical meta–double-bind of either/or thinking at Bateson's Learning Level II. In fact, Reason and Rowan (cited in in Douglass and Moustakas, 1985, p. 41) stated that "drive" or "commitment and attachment is encouraged." Indeed,

> researchers . . . down the years have started projects they really believed in . . . ideas they really cared about . . . too often these projects got pared down and chopped about and falsified in the process of getting ap-

> proval. . . . It doesn't have to be this way. Research doesn't have to be another brick wall. If we want to know about people, we have to encourage them to be who they are, and to resist all attempts to make them—or ourselves—into something we are not.
>
> [1981, p. xxiii]

It may be that, complementarily, dissonance decreased as the depth and duration of cybernetic shock increased. Heuristically, shock reversal involved immersion in a double-bind "Game Without End" by paradoxically immersing oneself in "playing" at turning one's back, on the pattern of either/or paradox—looking beyond to alternative views.

The "meta-search, the internal search to know" (Douglass and Moustakas, 1985, pp. 39–55), begins with the pattern of immersion (pattern involves meta-pattern) in the "field of study"; the "field" experience involved self-dialogue and self-exploration of the personal views and tacit knowledge that originated the inquiry. Specifically, in this study/inquiry, the heuristic essence found involved the pattern of Varela's formula (chapter 3, pp. 45–49): "being Ph.D./is the process of becoming Ph.D." (Keeney, 1983, p. 92).

As the researcher considered the patterns in the literature, other people, institutions, et cetera, the steps of the heuristic meta-search evolved and organized serendipitously, along the lines of the pattern of the following three-phrase model. Douglass and Moustakas (1985) outlined the approach as:

> 1. Immersion (exploration of the question, problem, or theme)
>   - Indwelling
>   - Internal frame of reference
>   - Self-search
> 2. Acquisition [collection of data]
>   - Tacit knowing
>   - Intuition
>   - Inference
>   - Self-dialogue [th-alk, th-lang]
>   - Self-disclosure
>   - Signitive-symbolic representation [See figures 1 through 7]
> 3. Realization [synthesis]
>   - Intentionality [interviews/dialogue]
>   - Verification [Intersubjectivity]
>   - Dissemination [Dissertation]
>
> [p. 47]

Immersion is described as the researcher's "total involvement in a research theme or question in such a way that the whole world is centered in it for a while" (Douglass and Moustakas, 1985, p. 47); the researcher's graduate studies involved a time frame of four years, as a complete participant observer. "Total involvement" in organized research began with the decision to take a "semi-sabbatical" to explore patterns and possible theme—a time frame of one year—begun in January 1987. Initially, the indwelling pattern of immersion manifested as "vague formless wanderings" (p. 47). From patterned internal frames of reference one is trying to catch a sense of meaning and direction in which perceptions and understanding match patterned external frames. Characteristic of this phase there was often a "feeling of lostness" (p. 47). As the self-search deepened, the researcher's Experiential Log indicated a vague pattern: "World View—as a 'targeted theme.' The 'target and theme' keep moving around!" For four to five months (even to this writing!) any reference to world view struck sensitive research chords, i.e., newspapers, journals, TV, new publications, conversations, and the chaotic "solitude" of "th-alk." Any call for a *change of world view* reverberated and nourished the search. Heuristic re-search involved the reintegration of derived knowledge of Learning I and II, welled up in patterns of "difficult to express in words or speech, implied or indicated but not actually expressed" tacit knowledge. Tacit knowing launched a pre-patterned way of becoming and exposed alternative Learning III paths to being and re-cognizing one's self as coming to know a pattern of "tricks" of a cybernetic epistemology. One trick involved declining participation in the "Game Without End," avoiding time and again getting caught up in the paradoxical double-bind of either/or, eternal contraries of Level II learning. Immersion, according to Douglass and Moustakas (1985), is the pattern of preparation and incubation required for furthering heuristic processes (p. 48).

Clearer patterns of acquisition occurred at some unspecified point in May ('87), when there was experienced a clear "sense of *direction* in which the theme or question is moving and [one] will know what is required to illuminate it . . . [thus] the time is right for collection of 'data' " (p. 48). The primary pattern is set: "When we know a thing from our own experience, its meaning can be recognized in others, without . . . accountings and explanation" (p. 51). "Direction" is the key word in the first of these statements. For the movement of theme and questions tended to behave like the patterns of quarks (Briggs and

Peat, 1984, pp. 77–9), described in subatomic research—one knows they're there—and there they are again. The dilemma was *how* to illuminate the patterns of experience of "knowing" what can't be seen. Tacit knowing, intuition, and inference converged, yielding glimmerings of vague, yet-to-be unified pictures. Self-dialogue, the "th-alk and th-lang" of the self-search of immersion, came from internal frames of reference and indwelling; all took on Polanyi's (1967) experienced, often misunderstood, "tacit knowledge" as their guide (cited in Douglass and Moustakas, 1985).

Intersubjectivity was sought in deep, sensitive interchanges of facilitative self-disclosure—fitting the pattern of "structure coupling" (Maturana, 1975, 1978). Or as Ferguson (1980) put it, there is the pattern of how one seeks to "conspire, with others in the sense of breathing together" (p. 19) as "knowing" the tricks of cybernetic epistemologists.

In the acquisition phase of heuristic inquiry meta-processes persist; however, they "take a backseat" to patterned collection of data, grounded in theory, as the formal review of the literature began. In addition to the Experiential Log of immersion, a reference catalog file was created from the review of literature and tacit dimensions. (Immersion according to heuristic inquiry is the forerunner of intuition and inference.) For the next three months (May through July 1987), during a period of intense study/work, the patterns of "key concepts" and phrases in the literature served as clues connecting the theme and ensuing questions listed later in the text (p. 103). As a heuristic attitude of openness to new *information* grew, the scope of inference seemed dangerously broadened. "Passionate commitment" gave voluminous access to the quality and bearing of emergent data, deemed as *necessary,* to include and reveal *all* the phenomena effectively. Once again, focusing and differentiation, the necessary "parameter" tools used in the identification of the theme and the pattern of "focused" question formulations, were put to use. Refocused, myriad patterns took form as a cognitive-body theoretically coupling the historical traditional, residual, and emergent conceptual frames with patterned Logical Learning Levels change (Bateson, 1972).

Heuristic Inquiry (Douglass and Moustakas, 1985) "permits shifts in method. . . . It is appropriate to change methods or procedure in midstream, according to the requirements of explicating the levels of meaning connected with the investigation" (p. 45). The sub-patterns of acquisition, tacit knowing, intuition, inference, self-dialogue (th-alk and th-lang), and data collected from the review of related literature took form as written self-disclosure linked the theoretical assumptions of chapter 2. Chapter 2 parallels the organization pattern of the text of the Experiential Log. Focus and differentiation became "drawing distinctions and punctuating" the "Whose and What" of world views change. Rychlak's (1981) textbook position on the pattern of personality theory's perspectives as based on Lockean or Kantian meta-assumptions fit as a *traditional* frame. The overriding paradox of Locke's constellation, the meta–double-bind of either/or thinking (Bateson's Learning II) steered the focus toward the pattern of the *residual* view of Kuhn's (1962, 1970) "Revolutions as Change of World View" (pp. 111–35). Becvar's (1986) circular revolution model and the introduction to a cybernetic epistemology gave further focus and differentiation to the framed pattern of questions: "When, Where, Why, and How" world view changes. Paradigm shift of the residual and traditional frames seemed linked by an overarching conflict paradigm—bound up by the recursive patterns of paradoxical meta–double-bind of either/or thinking.

The patterned illustrations of chapter 2 (figures 1–7) were heuristic "signitive-symbolic-representations," involved in the extension of the researcher's *emergent* patterns of the experience of data collections—"creating combinations and recombinations, sifting and sorting . . . moving in and out of appearance looking, listening carefully for meanings within meanings, attempting to identify the overarching qualities . . . at the heart of a new reality" (Douglass and Moustakas, 1985, p. 52). Bateson (1972, 1979, 1987), Varela, and Keeney (1983) helped challenge, yet they synthesized "versus" views revealing reciprocal tricks of a cybernetic epistemology. Cognitive dissonance (Festinger, 1957) lies at a level of recursion with Learning II—with paradox—the "eternal contraries" of recursive systems. Levels of recursion and orders of change presented the chaotic pattern of "cybernetic shock." Bateson (1972) had suggested that

> the creature is driven to level III by "contraries" generated at level II . . . resolving of these contraries will constitute positive reinforcement at level III. . . . Such resolution can take many forms. Level III can be dangerous . . . some fall by the wayside . . . labeled by psychiatry as psychotic . . . inhibited from using the first person pronoun.*
>
> [pp. 305–306]

At this point patterns of inference and intuition lead to the uncomfortable wondering if one *constructs* one's involvement "in a purposeless drift," Maturana's theory described, eternally "bouncing" from dissonance to shock. The "craziness" of Learning III and the dissonance at

*Excerpts from STEPS TO AN ECOLOGY OF MIND by Gregory Bateson, copyright © 1972 by Harper & Row, Publishers, Inc., reprinted by permission of the publisher.

Learning II that drives one there tug both beyond—and back to tacit knowing. One faces a "self"-constructed "brick-wall" of research referred to previously. Bateson's (1972) examples drove home dangers inherent in relying on a singular path of tacit knowledge

> the resolution of the contraries may be a collapsing of much that was learned at level II revealing a simplicity in which hunger leads directly to eating, and the identified self is no longer in charge of organizing the behavior. These are the incorruptible innocents of the world (p. 306).

Patterns of acquisition and immersion merge in the "beyond" territory of a cybernetic epistemologist's learning *about* learning at Level III. Jantsch (1980), von Foerster, and Maturana (as "invented by Segal" [1986]) fulfilled an *emergent* framework. A cybernetic epistemologist's trick of a *holding* pattern of "non-participation" in a Game Without End provides positive reinforcement in that it acts to increase alternative patterns. See "therapeutic triangulation," illustrated as figures 6 and 7 of this study (Broderick, 1983).

Moreover, according to Douglass and Moustakas (1985), "ultimately all knowledge and understanding," which in a sense is visionary, is incorporated in the tacit dimension. The "aesthetic and artistic" patterns that connect clues of organized cognition for the author of this study are found in the patterned illustrations, Figures 6 and 7 when identified, described, and demonstrated took a flexible position of "Therapeutic Triangulation." Thus imaged and illustrated, as models, they were no longer tacit; they came into awareness as a newly constructed alternative reality. Unfurled they recorded the patterns of experience, of internal sifting and altered behavior; an alternative route followed to resolve dissonance and recover from cybernetic shock.

Douglass and Moustakas (1985) described the decisive phase of heuristic inquiry as realization, where "a whole is assembled from the fragments and disparate elements that have been generated during the search for essence and meaning" (p. 52). Its synthesis is not a recap or summation. Rather, it is the "becoming" challenging examination of all the collected data and constructed models in combinations and recombinations, using tricky non-exhaustive patterns of a cybernetic epistemologist involving linear, circular, recursive, self-referential, paradoxical, and autonomous "data." The data are filtered and sorted in the search for meanings and meta-meanings and the attempt to reach the "overarching [autonomous] qualities that inhere in the data" (p. 52), an exploration of heuristic patterns that connect the organization of change of world view.

Heuristic Un-Methodological

Realization of heuristic inquiry (Douglass & Moustakas, 1985) involves illuminating the theme and questions through a patterned meta-search process (pp. 39–55). "Intentionality" is to "move from the specific to the general, from individuals to universals, from appearance to what is essence" as the theme, patterns, and organization of models seem to take on a "life of their own" (p. 53). The questions formulated, re-search began with patterns of "something that calls out from the challenges and attractions of significant experience . . . [face validity] revealed experientially through the researcher's own pattern of internal processes and those of intimate collaborators" (p. 53); those who would "conspire" or structure couple in the construction of a "new reality" (Douglass and Moustakas, 1985), as respondents engaged in dialogue in focused re-search interviews.

Whereas the process of heuristic inquiry began with the patterns of immersion and acquisition of theoretical data, there is an often misunderstood affirmation of initial grounding that has its organizing root patterns in the "self." The self as source from which a study/inquiry originates moves finally to explore the nature of others' patterns of experiences. Verification and dissemination were sought in intersubjectivity. The Institutional Review Board (IRB) approved protocol (IRB #4800, June 18, 1987) allowed the researcher a single ninety-minute audiotaped focused interview with volunteer respondents. The respondents included adult students enrolled in their final semester of doctoral study. A sample, representative of the gender balance of students in the program ($N = 7$, 5 females and 2 males) was recruited from the population ($n = 67$ [approximately a 2: 1 ratio of females to males]) by a request for volunteers (appendix B), posted on bulletin boards, handed out by the researcher and in classes with permission of instructors.

The inclusion criteria for respondents involved being a doctoral student in the major area of Individual, Marriage, and Family Development and Therapy and/or having completed the course Advanced Individual, Marriage and Family Development and Therapy (ED 145-665).

The respondents were questioned in dialogue during a private focused interview conducted by the investigator. Appendix C provides the general pattern of the focused interview schedule. (See pp. 000–00 for sample of questions.)

The parameters measured reflect a synthesis of the patterns of subjective-dependent experiences of being a doctoral student in Individual, Marriage and Family Development and Therapy. Data synthesis was accomplished by the researcher and was reported in aggregate form, to define patterns, categories, and themes that characterize the patterns of process involved in change of world view—or becoming a cybernetic epistemologist.

The foreseeable risks to respondents were spelled out in the consent form (appendix A). There were no risks involved for respondents other than those that may have been involved with increased self-awareness, which can also serve as a benefit. The benefits included a more in-depth knowledge of the patterns of educational process for these graduate students of Individual, Marriage and Family Development and Therapy.

The possible benefits to society included useful information and insights that may guide further research and inquiry and increase the base of understanding and knowledge in this area.

Respondents at any time during the study had the alternative of nonparticipation.

Confidentiality and anonymity were protected as follows: The name and identity of respondents were known only to the researcher. The information and insights secured were protected by the researcher according to the Institutional Review Board (IRB) approval #4800, June 18, 1987. In addition, the information was protected by the researcher according to the guidelines set forth in the Ethical Principles of the American Psychological Association and the Code of Ethics of the National Association of Social Workers. A master list assigning code numbers to letters was used for researcher identification of tapes and/or written notes and log. The master list was destroyed by the researcher at the end of the investigation. IRB had approved the retainment of all other data for a period of seven years after the completion of research, after which it will be destroyed (January 1, 1995).

The research "team" involved the literature review writings of the authors listed in the bibliography, faculty and advisers, peer/colleagues, the respondents, and the researcher interacting in the context of graduate education.

Research Summary

The following summary illuminates the theme and findings inherent in the various sections of the review of the literature. In chapter 2 and the final chapter 4 attempts were made to reach what Douglass and Moustakas (1985) refer to as the "overarching qualities that inhere in the data" (p. 52). *The major finding was: there are overarching patterns that connect epistemological change of world view.*

Heuristic inquiry's purpose, according to these scientists/scholars, is toward illuminating the theme and questions in a meta-search—emphasis is on patterned "reflective learning"—in that "reflection is a process of creating and clarifying the meaning of experience in terms of self in relation to self and self in relation to others" (p. 40). Babbie (1983) indicated qualitative methods generally have "more validity but less reliability" than empirical patterned quantitative methods and "results cannot be generalized as safely [p. 270]; . . . conclusions are seen as tentative rather than definitive" (p. 140).

The findings generally hinged on experiential resolution of the dualistic pattern of dissonance at Learning II involved with the overarching assumptions of Locke: demonstrative reasoning and either/or thinking—the paradoxical meta–double-bind of versus views—a conflict paradigm. Resolution of the patterns of *cybernetic shock* involved the experience of trying tricks of *knowing* a cybernetic epistemology; it involved construction of patterns that connect the organization of the researcher's personal experience in figures 6 and 7 (therapeutic triangulation)—as illustrated, an ecological patterning attempt at Learning III. The conceptual framework of three dimensions (traditional, residual, emergent and beyond) clarified the parameters of the theme of change of world view. Generally, I found from the review of the literature that:

- The philosophical/historical pattern of traditional conflicting world views of Locke and/or Kant provide the base for personality theory and are involved in patterns of epistemology—*how* one knows, thinks, and decides.
- Research and study of the pattern of meta-assumptions of traditional world views of the 17th century, Locke versus Kant, constructs a "battlefield" of conflict. The most profound is Cartesian Dualism—the basis of long-standing patterns of paradoxical either/or thinking—invisibly binding both personality and epistemology for over three centuries.
- Residual patterns of "Revolutions as Change of World View" perpetuate the dominant pattern of a conflict paradigm. Paradigm shift, described as cybernetic, is a pattern of circularity, part of a partial arc, one-half of a complementary recursive paradoxical pattern of either/or thinking; there is *no change* in a pattern of shifting problems to a *"left-handed complimentary"* or opposite frame.

- Sociocultural processes and a priori intellect, both/and, reconstitute patterned process or gauge one's world view. Change of world view, for this study, involved the pattern of learning to learn *about* learning (L. III), using a "Bootstrapper's" approach (Chew cited in Capra, 1983, pp. 93–94) and exploring patterns that connect the theme of change.
- A rapidly changing world has still retained remarkably stable patterned 17th century world views—alive and well in the latter part of the 20th century.
- Dissonance involved the pattern of conflict inherent in traditional and residual views. Dissonance lies at Bateson's problem solving Learning Level II, a cybernetic epistemology and the shock of complexity at Level III. Heuristic inquiry provided a resolution of dissonance map; its legend became: "Look for the Patterns That Connect a Theme of Change of World View."

This study/inquiry represents a beginning attempt to delineate the theme of world view change. It may be a very preliminary account of the nature of patterned cognition and how change of world view occurs. For as Bateson (1979) held, "changes in basic epistemology, character, self, and so on . . . involve shifting our whole system. . . . We must pass through the threat of that chaos where thought becomes impossible." Paradoxically, Bateson held "change will require various sorts of relaxation or contradiction within the system" (p. 143). One example Bateson (1972) gave cited Blake, who held "Without Contraries there is no progression," to which Bateson added, "Elsewhere I have called these contradictions at level II double-binds" (p. 303). In *Angels Fear* (1987), Bateson's daughter (coauthor) included a chapter credited to her deceased father titled "Let Not Thy Left Hand Know (GB)" (pp. 69–81). The inference to a pattern of "left-handed complimentarity" of Level III's "information" (the patterning difference that makes a difference) implied the *drive* of

> Learning II acquired in infancy is likely to persist through life. . . . Learning II is learning *to* learn; "deutero-learning"; "set learning"; "transfer of learning"; "reversal learning"; [and] appears . . . a necessary preparation for behavioral disturbance . . . [and/or] experimental neurosis. Selfhood is a product or aggregate of Learning II. Learning III is likely to be difficult and rare . . . there is a profound reorganization of character
>
> [1972, pp. 293–304]

Bateson and Bateson (1987) implied that Level II patterns of recursive paradoxical sacred "secrets [are] perhaps designed to be revealed" (p.

87). Paradoxically, the pattern of revelation quoted was: "Those who talk don't know, and those who know don't talk" (p. 10).

Recently, Carl Sagan (1988, February 7, *St. Louis Post-Dispatch, Parade,* pp. 4–7) identified "The Common Enemy" as "[political] revolutionaries who accomplished the impossible . . . entrenched for centuries. . . . What will it take to free us from the deadly trap that we have set for ourselves?" He lamented "the common enemy within us will be too strong for us to recognize and overcome. . . . Perhaps we will destroy ourselves." The Soviet Union and the United States are paradoxically asked to enact a supposedly new recursive pattern of: "compete in cooperativeness," with an attitude and pre-patterned process of "glasnost and perestroika [openness and restructuring]." He wondered: "Are we at last coming to our senses and beginning to work together on behalf of the species and the planet?" Or as von Foerster's ethical imperative edicts have we realized: " 'A' is better off, when 'B' is better off" (cited in Segal, 1986, p.4). Chapter 4 verifies and disseminates this heuristic inquiry's all important pattern of realization. The factor of graduate students' involvement in complex Learning II and III changes—on their becoming cybernetic epistemologists.

Suggestions for Further Research

The findings presented suggest topics and heuristic questions for further research. Cognitive theory holds that there is a pattern of "irrational belief systems" (Ellis, 1975) as part of one's world view, which can be challenged by disputing disturbing self-talk, the th-alk and th-lang involved in the patterns of the experience of dissonance. In order to change one's irrational beliefs or negative view of self, others, and/or the world, one must first recognize precisely *what* that pattern of beliefs or world view is, i. e., "Perfectionism, Procrastination, Discomfort Anxiety, and/or Low Frustration Tolerance." Ellis (1975) based his cognitive-behavioral therapy (Rational-Emotive Therapy or RET) on cognitive theory and on the principle of Epictetus (first century A.D.). "People are not disturbed by things, but the views which they take of them." An upsetting "Emotional Episode" is patterned as the "ABC's" of RET: A = an Activating event; B = Beliefs about the event; C = Consequent feelings associated with the Evaluative th-alk and th-lang going on as one constructs their view of the world, self and/or other as 100% "AWFUL or TERRIBLE!" Perspective, or point of view, has to do with the view coming "outside-in" (behavioristic). Epistemology, *how* one thinks, knows, and decides, is a patterned process "inside-out," akin to studies in both constructivism and structure determinism.

Further research could be on the early-in-life development of the patterns of cognition—or epistemology. How do infants assimilate, nominalize, prioritize, ordinalize, intervalize, correlate, et cetera? Language and cognitive development in children seem to follow closely the patterns of the Statistical Order of Measurement Scaling: (1) Nominal (Naming, Ma-Ma, Da-Da, baby); (2) Ordinal (Mine! Me first!); (3) Interval (take turns or alternate); (4) Ratio (sharing). Constructivists (Segal, 1986) held we do not know how the brain works: "all brains perform computation" (p. 84). Cognitive therapy might say one *computes* in patterns to a "reasonably contented ratio" by keeping an "improper" balance of $\frac{\text{intellect}}{\text{emotion}}$. Bateson's (1972) Learning Level "changes," Zero to IV, seem to correlate with this mathematical scaling order—that is, Learning III and IV might take one to statistical heights presently unknown; as in this study, progressivly larger geometric patterns could be involved.

Finally, taking Bateson's (1979) lead: "The wider perspective—is *about* perspectives," much can be learned from further exploration and study on the patterns that connect organizational world view perspectives/epistemologies—their root patterns almost certainly go deeper than Greek philosophy and earlier myth. Bateson further emphasized the immediate dangers of a pattern of conflict/revolution perspective: "I believe that the myth of *power* always corrupts, because it proposes a false, though conventional, epistemology . . . such metaphors lead us to grope in the wrong direction" (Hannon, 1986, p. 50). Submission is the reciprocal pattern of power—you can't have one without the other. It might well be humankind's patterned eternal quest to control elements in Nature one can never control that leads to the paradoxical recursive pattern of addiction/dependency: In the duel to prove oneself more powerful than substances/control one is ultimately dependent/controlled *by* them.

A related timely topic is values education. From what is known about the patterns of value systems, its connection to change of world view is intimate. It is hoped that this study might serve as a resource or pattern for development of academic courses on values and/or ethics. The researcher encourages its application and use, as well as consenting to adaptation of its concepts to fit any grade level.

Chapter 4, the final chapter, deals first with the study/inquiry according to the pattern of the review of the literature. It originates from the perspective/epistemology of student factors—as the pattern of synthesis for essence and meaning begins. Then it moves on, following the internal patterns of reflection on epistemological cybernetic shock. Finally, the inquiry ends with the patterns of verbatim responses of intimate collaborator respondents whose focused interviews—on becoming dialogues—fit the conceptual theme of a cybernetic epistemology, a pattern that connects a change of world view—beyond revolution.

CHAPTER 4

Student Factors—Cybernetic Shock (Meta-for)

Literature Review

Related to the patterns of process, of learning *about* learning, there is significant correlation between Learning III and "becoming a cybernetic epistemologist." Keeney (1983) related that "the trick is to . . recognize patterns . . . recursive or cybernetic . . . [and] acknowledge that we always have been cybernetic epistemologists" (p. 60). Knowing *how* is tricky. Re-cognition of recursive and *emergent* metapatterns of organization in this study has prompted model construction, yet

> As we have seen from the beginning . . . while metaphors may offer a temporary insight into a complex system, they are necessarily limited, sometimes gravely so. A model is never the thing it stands for. Nevertheless, models and metaphors have a tendency to assume a life of their own
>
> [Briggs and Peat, 1984, p. 238].

Pattern-wise, Carl Whitaker (1975), known for his "Psychotherapy of the Absurd" and his a-theoretical stance, warned: "Never marry a hypothesis, and be cautious when dating a theory" (pp. 154–64). Whitaker's "absurd" warning has generated Makinnon and Slives (1984) to question, "If One Should Not Marry a Hypothesis . . . Should One Marry a Model?" (Pp. 26–39.) As these patterned absurdities and the study attempt to point out, "models" and metaphors conjure enduring images (Chinese proverb: "One picture is worth a thousand words"), assume lives of their own, and become outdated and abused—posing a danger in their "mestastability" over time and space (C. Bateson, 1985, p. 45; Jantsch, 1980, p. 17; see block quotation p. 59, "Evolution—Revolution").

In this study it is hypothesized (1) that a student in the major area of Individual, Marriage and Family Development and Therapy, having been trained in the necessity for patterned empirical truths and understanding, will experience cognitive dissonance or discomfort and psychological tension (Festinger, 1957) as well as confusion and concern in the process of *becoming* and/are introduced to cybernetic epistemology. Furthermore, (2) in the patterns of process of learning, a graduate student may become aware of puzzling anomalies that result in a crisis in thinking, or *cybernetic shock,* as the pattern of paradigm shift occurs. The duration and degree of the patterns of cybernetic shock undoubtedly vary from student to student and are a focus of this study/inquiry. Fundamentally, it is hypothesized that a shift to cybernetic epistemology is experienced as a *revolution* in thinking comparable to Kuhn's (1962, 1970) description of paradigm shifts in the scientific community. Bateson (1972) held: "Learning II occurs whenever there is measurable learning *about* the fact of reversal. . . . Learning II ["problem solving" and "selfhood"] is a learning of the contexts of Learning I" (p. 302). Level III is learning *about* the contexts of contexts (cybernetics of cybernetics of cybernetics.).

Early on, through *residual* educational contexts of primary, secondary, and undergraduate learning as well as sociocultural processes, a student population has been socialized in a patterned epistemology of linear dichotomies and cause/effect thinking—based on processes of objective competition and revolutionary conflict toward progress and growth. These historically dominant patterned views served well as long as "growth" remained a desirable factor.

However, according to the *St. Louis Post-Dispatch* (May 16, 1988), the growth of world population is now

> Imperiling Earth. . . . World population, now 5.1 billion, grew by an precedented 90 million people last year. . . . Over the next 10 years, the world will add another billion people. . . . Understand that competition for food and resources of this planet will become more intense."

Emerging at the graduate level, a student in Individual, Marriage and Family Development and Therapy is expected to make the process shift to a cybernetic epistemology. At this point, it is hypothesized, the recursive pattern of dissonance manifests itself. Dissonance leaves one logically trying to re-solve reversible patterns of perceptual conflicts. In other words, it is as if everything one has previously learned does not fit—and suddenly everything seems related and relevant. The patterns of cybernetic shock overlap dissonance; its depth and duration undoubtedly vary from student to student. It manifests somewhat like sociological future shock or the symptoms of psychological shock. Dissonance leaves some logically trying to make consonant patterned perceptual conflicts at an objective level of previous seemingly irrelevance of fit. At higher levels of synthesis [Learning III] the patterns and view get "fuzzy." Generally, a student is found "wandering between two world [views], one dead, the other powerless to be born" (T. S. Eliot, "'43/'73," p. 59; cited in Keeney, 1983, p. 11).

Faced with dissonance of this scope, a student may manifest differing degrees of *cybernetic shock*. Bateson (1972) held: "Learning II will simplify the universe by handling [contrary] instances as a *single category*. But if Learning II is concerned with the contexts of these instances, then the categories of Learning II burst open" with L. III (p. 305), as in the dilemma of complement and *left-handed compliment*.

Student factors of dissonance and shock were empathically portrayed by various sources in a review of the literature. Bronowski (1978) in a *residual* frame offered:

> wars and credibility gaps . . . in the end come down to this: growing up in university communities . . . [generates and maintains the] feeling that we trust people to say just what they think. We believe that they will tell the truth . . . honesty, integrity, dignity are respected. We are very disappointed when it happens not to be so. When I meet university students, I am conscious of the fact they do not think that there is a credibility gap, they just think it is a hypocrisy gap . . . you, the elders, are allowed to practice a form of hypocrisy, which they are not allowed to practice within the hallowed halls of universities.
>
> [pp. 134—35]

Macmillian and Garrison (1984) addressed the problem patterns of *traditional/residual* research traditions in education and the critical stance, from the standpoint of a student's "redescription and interpretation," or the reliability of subjective (objective) statements. From an educative stance:

> Any critic must re-describe the object of his criticism. This is done by giving quotations, restructuring arguments, examining the literature, and so forth. Description, though, shades off into interpretation as the critic selects passages, winnows out assumptions, and so forth. . . . [The most] arrogant assumption is that empirical scientists must always satisfy philosophical standards of rigor and precision in their ongoing research and, theory development. . . . an opposite view—that because philosophy is a handmaiden of science, the philosopher, should have the humility of a charwoman—is no more palatable. . . . current research tradition ought to be one of mutual respect; . . . approaching the ideals of dialectic.
>
> [p. 20]

Kuhn (1962, 1970) reported Einstein's experience of paradigm shift being "as if the ground had been pulled out from under one" (p. 83) without a patterned paradigmatic theory to build on. Further, he cited James's account of a " 'bloomin' buzzin' confusion" (p. 114), that perceived experience pattern has taught students to see, during paradigm shift. Kuhn noted the neglect of sixties gestalt experiments on the pattern of perceptual transformations during paradigm shifts (pp. 112—13). Fortuitously, according to Kuhn (1962, 1970), students when confronted with anomalies bordering on crisis take different attitudes. There is the chaotic pattern of "proliferation of competing articulations, a willingness to try anything, the expression of explicit discontent, the recourse to philosophy and debate over fundamentals, all these are the symptoms of a transition to extraordinary research" (p. 91). Or some students choose, during the crisis phase of *revolution as* "change," and/or are directed to "pick up the other end of the stick," i.e., handle the same data using a different frame (p. 85). Kuhn wrote that students who are introduced to a new world view, having completed paradigm shift as a result of complete pattern gestalt conversion switch,

> see new and different things when looking . . . in places they have looked before. It is as if . . . they had been suddenly transported to another planet where familiar objects are seen in a different light . . . and joined by familiar ones as well. . . .
>
> Transformations [are] usually more gradual and almost always irreversible—are common concomitants of scientific training. . . . At times of revolution . . . the scientist must learn to see a new gestalt . . . must be re-educated. . . . After . . . the world of his research will seem incommensurable with the one he has inhabited before . . . schools guided by different paradigms are always slightly at cross-purposes*
>
> [pp. 111–12]
> [Experienced as dissonance.]

Both Bronowski (1978) and Kuhn (1962, 1970) wrote of cumulative residual "error built on error" and deletions of "laundered" texts. The scientific task, according to Kuhn, "is to invent concepts—yet there is a *pattern* of historical mistakes that misleads both students and laymen about the nature of scientific enterprise" (p. 142). This factor Kuhn (1962, 1970) attributed to "The Invisibility of Revolutions" (pp. 136–44). Paradoxically, he stated, "in the case of textbooks, there are even good reasons why . . . they should be systematically misleading" (p. 137). The ahistorical, non-contextual, "pedagogical arsenal that makes a man a scientist . . . is immensely successful" (p. 141); "the scientist's world is quantitatively and qualitatively enriched" (p. 7).

**The Structure of Scientific Revolutions* (Chicago: University of Chicago Press, 1962, 1970), © 1962.

It seems crystal clear that blame has been dumped into the pool of *traditional/residual* educational processes and its institutions. Yet personality theory may also deserve criticism, as a quote from the unnamed dean of a "prominent graduate school" noted:

> There is the question of what graduate school can do for people aged 25 or so, after family, church, college and other influences have had an impact. Can you make fundamental changes in the students' standards? You are dealing with a formed personality.
> [*St. Louis Post-Dispatch,* May 24, 1987, Editorial page].

Bateson (1979) suggested the *residual* patterned "facts of dee obsolescence" of current educational processes are a "rip-off" from the standpoint of students. From the *traditional* frame, he related

> William Blake saw that the philosophy of *Locke* and *Newton* could only generate "dark Satanic mills . . . " every aspect of our civilization is *split* wide open . . . capitalist [vs.] communist—and we are told that we *must* take sides in the struggle between two monstrous ideologies. In the business of thinking, we are torn between . . . try[ing] to run a university and to maintain standards of "excellence" in the face of growing distrust, vulgarity, insanity, exploitation of resources, victimisation of persons, and quick commercialism. . . . The screaming voices of greed, frustration, fear and hate . . . the same old *dualistic pragmatism.* [italics added]
> [p. 218]

Students are as obsolete as teachers, said Bateson (1979). He offered a "lethal" dose to patterns of conflicting views and rigid complementarities or symmetries. It is time to realize that time is running out. He called dualistic rigor versus imagination (objective versus subjective) "two great contraries of mental processes, either of which by itself is lethal. Rigor is paralytic death, but imagination alone is insanity" (p. 219). By now, he wrote, there is the recognition of the recursive pattern of polarity relationships that presents a problem of combination; the question is how to proceed. For starters he suggested "rising above partisanship"—and a kind of individual statesmanship that considers any and all duty as "non-trivial" (p. 222).

Bateson (1979) believed: "The wider perspective is *about* perspectives" (p. 223). First, *how* one views the world involves "what" one sees, and then vice versa. Metaphors, in the form of models and language, symbolize and have patterned likenesses to something else. Therefore, reciprocally, metaphors and language symbolize patterns of epistemology or world view. Power words and battle metaphors (revolution) are "to be distrusted . . . [are] dangerous" and seem "in the [life-] boat called" 1988 to have outlived their usefulness—having more than a few perilous, gaping holes. In a nuclear-accident/war prone world outdated symbols and metaphors pose extreme danger. War is no longer resolutory; its future cost patterns have become unqualifiably unquantifiable. Bateson (1979) asked only that teachers dispel the "*myth of 'power'*" (p. 223) and combat.

Douglas (1976) held the patterned perspective of perspectives as "either/or," paradoxically, a "Classical (Cooperative) Paradigm of Society" or "The Conflict Paradigm of Society." Thus reflecting the cybernetic complexity involved in what *emergent and beyond* framed scientists are today referring to as patterns of "chaotic dynamics" or "Murphy's Law squared." That is, "Murphy's X Murphy's = chaotic dynamics" (J.J., Feigenbaum, *St. Louis Post-Dispatch,* July 8, 1978).

Both Segal (1986) and Keeney (1983) alluded to what von Foerster portrayed as the patterned traditional/residual processes and praxes of education as a "trivialization of students." This too seems to arise from the either/or paradox applied to a subjective versus objective perspective of the goals of socialization. (Praxis involves what is taught or done "to" the organism in processes of socialization.) According to von Foerster (Segal, 1986; Keeney, 1983), at first the organism and "its" world are completely subjective. Family, kindergarten, and the social milieu are not ready for this kind of unpredictable (child's unpatterned subjective-chaotic) takeover of the world. A singular (demonstrative) predictable view of the world is *the* objective and also *is* objective: it is the child's ticket for admission to society. Beginning with birth, or according to Kant, even before birth (long before formal education), pre-patterned process and praxis provide the organism with the correct answers to every question asked. Most of this is endless questioning is structured as the "trivial pursuit of learning." However, the closer objective views agree, the closer to patterned perfection all organisms interacting come to "perfect trivialization . . . symbolic of exemplary performances." That is, to offset the pattern of trivialization, von Foerster (cited in Keeney, 1983) would construct an educational system focused to ask "questions to which the answers are unknown" thereby, he held, tapping the huge reservoir of creative subjective experience of both students and teachers, involving them in a kind of Socratic dialogue (p. 79).

Segal (1986) specified "Trivial vs Non-trivial Machines," as von Foerster constructs: Trivial machines are patterned "predictable . . . history independent, . . synthetically and analytically determinstic (mechanistic)." By contrast, von Foerster pictured the pattern of the nontrivial machine as also "Synthetically deterministic . . . [yet] *historically dependent,* . . analytically *indeterminable* and *unpredictable* (organismic)" (pp. 107–109). The trivial machine epitomizes our quest for certainty and the patterned "wishes" for understanding, prediction and control, "Man" ultimately winning the eternal war with him/herself, others, and the environment.

A "flexible borderline for the essential abilities for intelligent behavior" (Hofstader, 1979) reframes the foregoing and Maturana's (1975) theoretical concept of "structure coupling"—the aesthetic cognitive art of "behaving with $\frac{\text{intelligence}}{\text{emotions}}$" (cited in Dell, 1985, pp. 1–20). Hofstadter (1979) held the following pattern of behaviors as essential:

- to respond to situations very flexibly;
- to take advantage of fortuitous circumstances;
- to make sense out of ambiguous or contradictory messages;
- to recognize the relative importance of different elements of a situation;
- to find similarities between situations despite differences which may separate them;
- to draw distinctions between situations despite similarities which link them;
- to synthesize new concepts by putting them together in new ways;
- to come up with ideas which are novel. [Hofstadter, 1979, p. 26]

Hofstadter (1979) further proposed that one of the major efforts (attempted by this study) of his book is to

> urge each reader to confront apparent contradition head on, to savor it, to turn it over, to take it apart, to wallow in it, so that in the end . . . emerge with new insights into the seemingly unbreachable gulf between the formal and the informal, the animate and the inanimate, the flexible and the inflexible.
>
> [p. 16]

Keeney (1983) provocatively told of an illicit "quiet *revolution*" involving the sciences and humanities, promising a transformation of epistemology, the way we think, know and decide, implying a pattern of shift to validate subjective experiential views (p. 4). Similarly, Ferguson (1980) too, drew a picture of the *revolution* having its "front within, a play within a play"; she too imaged an arced pattern of transformative shifts as "pendulum shifts that have become paradigm change" (pp. 71–73). An organized pattern of misplaced strategic interventions is aimed at social institutions then families, then the individual . . . then institutions in vicious circular patterns round a rigid pathological triangle that involves the view that individual/family/social institutions are to blame and "should" change, trying the same "old" epistemological pattern of "tricks" of restructuring and reorganizing in a pattern of first order "solutions that maintained problems" for past generations. According to Ferguson (1980): "Lives have become *revolutions*"; she continued, progressing around the pathological "schismogenic" triangle, targeting the individual in the pattern who is at the brink of *conversion to a new world view* as beginning "in earnest," ready to re-construct everything. Seeing the light, each individual looks "anew" at the patterns of personal work, relationships, health, political power, and "experts' views." Individual questionable "goals and values" become the adversaries at the "front within" (p. 24). However, Ferguson cautioned in *The Aquarian Conspiracy* (1980):

> Someone is always trying to summon us back to dead allegiance: Back to God, the simple-minded religion of an earlier day. 'Back to basics,' the simple-minded education. Back to simple-minded patriotism . . . called back to simple-minded 'rationality' contradicted by personal experience and frontier science.
> [p. 128]

Thus Ferguson (1980) implied there are no simple or poetic answers of "complete simplicity" involved in the sequel to the "Age of Aquarius." Jantsch (1980) similarly represented this traditional conceptual pattern as the "summoning back" to simple solutions of complex problems as "re-ligio." Like the Tantra in Buddhism, "a return to origins," in his view, however, involves an attempt to strengthen "sacred" meaning in the complex patterns of process (p. 311).

As McCulloch (cited in Keeney, 1983) directed, the author asks, "Don't bite my finger, look where I am pointing" (p. 61). It is part of the involvement of this study to investigate what has been referred to in the literature as patterns of change involving "invisible, inward *revolutions*" in thinking. For *emergent* patterns turn them inside-out with new cybernetic epistemological "tricks." Still, as Keeney (1983) pointed out "one's epistemological 'slip' is always showing" (p. 22). For, as von Foerster narrated his constructivist's epistolary: "I am convinced that I was looking for it ["a constructed reality"] with my mind's eye all my life; I recognized when I saw it, and I clung to it with all my strength" (cited in Segal, 1986, p. 156). Moreover, he recounted a constructivist plan to address those

> puzzling and mystifying answers to simple and clear questions. . . . The trouble with the utterances of great men is that they are so transpar-

ent . . . paradoxically, what is transparent cannot be seen . . . my plan is to make . . . issues opaque so that they can be seen, at least for a moment, before they slip away when clarified.
[p. xiii]

Consequently, this study of students hypothesizes that patterns of cognitive dissonance and cybernetic shock occur in synchrony with the pattern of paradigm shift from a linear to a recursive world view . . . and into the "dangerous beyond territory" of Learning III. This review of the literature of student factors attempts to give some kind of new in-formation and pattern to enable one to make connections to the residual framed phenomenon Kuhn (1962, 1970) metaphorically called "Revolutions as Changes of World View" (pp. 111–35). In addition, the study provided a description and discussion of cybernetic epistemology as "a way of discovering and constructing alternative patterns in the ecology of our experience" (Keeney, 1983, p. 48). It is meant to give example to Bateson's (1972, 1979) process of "Learning III, or learning *about* Learning II" contraries, as the essence of becoming a cybernetic epistemologist. Beyond . . . (Learning II change) meta or overinclusive are the emergent complex patterns of a universal coevolutionary paradigm of Jantsch (1980), von Foerster's constructivism as invented by Segal (1986) and Maturana's (1978) structure determinism, which present organized patterns of "the complexity and elegance of autonomous and [sacred] interconnected patterns of life—a full[er] view." (Keeney, 1983, p. 109)

Finally, as cybernetic shock lifts, Bateson and Bateson (1987) offered the ultimate "epistemology of the sacred," as sequel—beckoning us to Learning III and IV—where heretofore even "angels feared to tread." *Cybernetic shock,* the hypothesized pattern of *confusion and concern* that ensues at Learning Level III change, according to Bateson and Bateson (1987), has secret patterns designed to be revealed (p. 87). The following section reflects this study's heuristic pattern of dissemination process, which involved exploration of this complex, sometimes dangerously chaotic learning level change of—becoming a cybernetic epistemologist.

Cybernetic Shock [Meta-for]

A Webster's (1983) definition of cybernetics reveals that the word derives from the Greek meaning "helmsman: the one who steers the ship." Epistemology, also of Greek derivation, is a "discussion of knowledge." It is depicted as a "branch of philosophy which investigates the origin and nature of knowledge." Further,

> it is a discipline distinct from logic, which has traditionally occupied itself with the mind's operation in the knowing process. With regard to the origin of knowledge, empiricism traces all knowledge to sense perception . . . rationalism insists that the mind contributes to knowledge certain general ideas not derived from experience . . . realism teaches that the object of knowledge is independently real . . . and idealism makes the object entirely, or in part, dependent on the mind's activity.
> [*Columbia Encyclopedia,* 1956, p. 626]

In other words, this study looks at the patterns of organization of the structural nature of cognition (steering knowledge)—as *who* steers the ship of knowledge of change/stability of world view? *What* cargo is packed away in the hold? *When* does the helmsman's watch change? *Where* does the ship "take on" its (value) cargo? *Why* is one cargo more "valuable" than another? And *how* does change of helmsman and/or cargo affect the voyage?

Patterns of cybernetic shock or confusion and concern manifests and involves cognitive dissonance (Festinger, 1957), "steering" in back and forth patterns to alien or real (knowledge) ports of mind's active processes. Dissonance is prerequisite cargo in that it provides the "uncomfortable psychological tension . . . of two or more [pre-patterned] cognitions that do not 'fit' together, according to psychological logic" (Reynolds, 1971, p. 39). (The following relates to chapter 2, "Traditional Framework—Seventeenth-Century World Views" and/or figures 1, 4, and 5 lists of exemplars.) The structure of a conflict paradigm has provided the vessel carrying a supposedly value-free cargo of dualistic either/or thinking. The *traditional* helmsman (Locke) leisurely steered the (value-) free ship of *Certainty* to and fro, since the 17th century. (See figure 1.) The ship's log indicates she had *two* home ports—Truth and Falsity. It has been written and proven by experienced experts that she demonstrated a most powerful preference for the free port of Truth. And it seems when she did venture out to find Falsity, it was only to prove, empirically, that Truth was where you found it, as it had been determined. *Certainty's* log held the figures to prove this. From the time she was launched, every voyage was carefully plotted, reduced to the factor of "the shortest distance between two points is a straight line." *Certainty* was a beauty to behold as she sat anchored in Truth. It was sad when reality made it necessary for her to set sail. Yet logged shakedown cruises had shown she was willing to mediate, if Truth were in jeopardy. This ship carried few passengers; the crew and view never changed. Even so, there was little or no competition for *Certainty* until Kant (about a century later) appeared far-out, barely visible by teloscope on the horizon. Kant's vessel seemed loosely structured to carry a cargo that was value-laden and varied with each voyage. Her name was *Uncertainty,* Kant metaphorically couldn't decide if he should compete, so he naturally steered in simple, understandable cybernetic circles around *Certainty* whenever she had to venture out. *Uncertainty* was always at sea. Steersman Kant held that access to the free port of Truth was as it appeared, when it is blocked by *Certainty.* He said "we need to talk about this man to man." He thought both Truth and Falsity were there and were somewhere else, beyond—or maybe there were other good and bad ports, but more good ones than meet the eye. Kant's crew and passengers were all-Pro (forma). In that they formed a happy-go-lucky group of people, yet their values seemed beyond reproach. They were always carrying on about transcending all ports—and optimistically believed the "best" place to be is right were you are, since it was felt ideally *you* will be there when you arrive. Critically, cruising around in dizzy circles aboard *Uncertainty,* one could never be *totally* certain where you would/had land(ed) or if you'd ever see land again. Booking passage on the Kantian Line required anchoring in deep introspective thought; with Locke predictably the course was visibly consistent, set out as a single straight course as to where to start and where to end up. Most people to this day, understandably and predictably prefer to book passage on the well-controlled ship of *Certainty;* pragmatically in a rapidly changing world one hasn't the time for destinations that may not be there at the time of arrival. ETA (Estimated Time of Arrival), too, is another dubious concern. Staying with the Lockean Line made real good sense as long as *Certainty* remained seaworthy and her crew could control her on 20th century theoretical seas of Change. *Certainty* always had a fifty-fifty chance of maintaining control, except when bravely foraging a sea of Change; then it was all she could do to maintain stability and control and she was seen sadly limping back to Truth by way of Reality. Given half a chance she might have made it had not quantum physics à la Einstein, Bohr, and Bell (Trefil, 1987, pp. 67–75) constructed invisible barriers of quarks found hidden in wave particle duality experiments. In 1935 Einstein-Podolsky-Rosen (EPR) constructed what is known as as the EPR paradox, theoretically poking holes in the by now dangerously leaky ship of *Certainty.* It had come to pass that Bell's Theorem (1960s) re-constructed a new ship of *Uncertainty Principle* that is so fast she "really is not any 'place' and is not there when you are not looking" (p. 67). *Uncertainty* still floats on late-20th-century seas of more complex *Cybernetic Shock.* A cargo of confusion and concern clearly manifests in the Universal seas traversed by *Uncertainty Principle*. Signalman First Class Trefil (1987) blinks an SOS from the "Quantum physics' world: now you see it, now you don't." As a theoretical physicist by trade, he expressed incredulously (about a cargo of quarks, et. al): "If you have to cope with atomic particles that can read your mind even when they don't exist, it can be hard to explain what you do" (p. 67) or where you'll end up *if* you get there!

Besides, late-twentieth-century cybernetic shock has to do with the inherent complexity of patterns of cybernetic epistemological (knowledge steering) processes of how one knows—and *knows* s/he knows. Epistemology as a concept seems better related to cognitive theory; perspective as a concept relates better with certain personality theory "states and traits." Cognition is *how* one views the world (inside-out). *What* one sees is perspective or "the view" (outside-in). There is a great deal of confusion and concern about staying afloat in chaotic cybernetic waters on the new seas of Shock as a passenger of *Uncertainty Principle*. Thus, this type of tossing about of concepts is characteristic of a pattern of becoming a cybernetic epistemologist; sincere communicative attempts at responsible description come out perceived as unpatterned, uncertain, free-associative muddle. Categorical patterns of organization can be lost in a sea disrupted by the tossing about of ideas of complexity. Paradoxically, they can be relocated near the surface or at the level of embarkation. Too, invented patterns can prove to be invisibly paradoxical—strange and "loopy."

In the *residual frame*, Kuhn (1962, 1970) held that change of world view is experienced as a "revolution." Historical and philosophical circular revolutions are paradoxically described as paradigm shifts. Shifts are neither cybernetic nor circular as Kuhn described, but patterns of partial arcs of large recursive binding patterns. There are nests of patterns, having been ineptly likened to Chinese boxes fitting serially into one another. There are micro-patterns, regular patterns, macro-patterns, meta- and meta-meta patterns, et cetera. Some patterns are clear; the "meta" you go, the less visibility. So there are patterns of patterns of patterns and so on; matching them up is bound to prove dissonance. Some patterns remain tightly closed to exploration and/or to any connections (that is, unless you're into embarkation on late-twentieth-century models of Uncertainty Principle). Thus the *residual* punctuation of the pattern of *revolutions* as *the* prescribed dynamic for any and all *change*. Metaphorically, revolution has settled to/as the bottom-line pattern for broad organizational change in micro and macro systems (Segal, 1986. p. 15). Centuries old patterns of the spirit of competition and conflict filtered out of traditional world views. Revolutions metaphorically bespeak an epistemology of conflict paradigm (either/or). As Keeney (1983) said, "one's epistemological 'slip' is always showing" (p 22), that is, how one views the world—as conflictual, co-operative, co-evolutional, or sacred. The "problem" remains threefold, as to what is the nature of one's th-lang, how to th-alk, and what is said. For with descriptions, "Everything that is said is said by an observer to another observer who may be him or herself" (Maturana, cited in Segal, 1986, p. 62).

One must fish for an *emergent* holding pattern that one is told lies in a pathological triad consisting of lines running beyond, between, and within. Bateson (1979) held "the wider perspective is *about* perspectives" (p. 223). He also related there is a profound difference between patterns of *shift* and *change,* between any

> serious attempt to change the characterological *state* of an organism and trying to change that organism's particular *actions.* The latter is relatively easy; [first order change]; the former, profoundly difficult. Paradigmatic change is as difficult as—indeed is of the same nature as—change in epistemology [second order change] [italics added].
>
> [p. 124]

Dissonance drives the making of a choice between conflicting world views bound by an invisible recursive steering paradoxical meta–double-bind that excludes choice—it is thereby schismogenic and constitutive of a Game Without End. Escape is perceived as in "craziness" and/or passive addiction (Bateson, 1972, p. 306), toward what Hampden-Turner (1981) and contemporaries of "catastrophe theory" held will be the death/annihilation of all matter (pp. 194–197).

The pattern for survival involves *emergent and beyond* contextual savvy; moves vary in the Game Without End: (1) Refuse to play—this is sometimes what is known as becoming "eclectic" or neutral, "dropping out," or shifting to the opposite frame. (2) Introduce another "game"—triangulate; this can prove dangerous, however, for games disguise their rules of recursion; it only takes two to play, in complementary, symmetrical, or parallel (reciprocal) "negative coalition" interchange circuits. (*3*) *Develop awareness of patterns that connect one's mind to the universe and each other.* This is the *ultimate trick,* for a game of complex levels changes—and may be applicable at what Bateson (1972) called Learning Level changes III and IV. This trick tends to be involved with the in-formed ('Information') patterns of one's own cognitive processes structured and coupling life and universe. From the pattern of th-alk and the nature of the th-lang as a pattern, a key is cut-to unlock the secrets of *why* and *how* one *copes, adapts,* or *changes* world view. The author's personal key concept involved computing and holding to a pattern of a "reasonably contented ratio" of INTELLECT: emotions. This pattern of pattern involves *how* and *why* one *becomes.* Becoming is an active game involving responses of others and the environment. It is a timely, serious newly re-structured and re-constructed responsible new form of process. Taken seriously, it leads to re-view and re-vision of creative HEURISTIC PATTERNS THAT CONNECT A CHANGE OF WORLD VIEW. (Unfortunately, a thorough understanding of this third trick means further study of the science of the patterns of organization presented herein and elsewhere.) It bears repeating here, "the 'Ph.D.'/is the process leading to 'Ph.D.' "

Meanwhile, cybernetic shock manifests itself with the complexity of reboarding the new ship of *Uncertainty Principle.* (1) *Universal emergent* views overarch (non-hierarchically) (A) versus views (conflict paradigm), (B) verses views (cooperative paradigm), with (C) a paradigm of co-evolving micro and macro systems and hints of therapeutic triangulation. (2) Structure determinism holds primarily that through responsible use of language an "objective" universe is replaced by a "multiverse, where many observer 'verses' co-exist, each valid in its own right" (Efram and Lukens, 1985, p. 25). (3) Constructivism holds "We CONSTRUCT or INVENT" a "lifeboat" we call "REALITY" (Segal, 1986, p. 17). Small wonder one's pattern of approach is tentative concerning change of "Lines" (Rosenthal, 1984, p. 118) on ways to maneuver about in the world. Confusion calms, somewhat paradoxically, in (1/C—see above) the "domain of self-organizing system[s]. Information is [found as] also capable of organizing itself; new knowledge arises" (Jantsch, 1980, p. 11). Yet sincere dubious concern persists, steering a cybernetic epistemologist's thoughts toward a new ship of *Meta-Matters;* reboarding is by way of Bateson's dizzying "zig-zag ladder of analysis." *Meta-Matters's* course seems set heading one into a sea of Chaos and Discontent. The secret passage, according to Catherine Bateson's collaboration on her father's posthumous unpublished writings, is little used. In the past, it is written that "angels feared" these "sacred" seas of Epistemology. Their honesty fosters further concern and discontent, in that the Batesons revealed their "book can tell you nothing unless you know nine-tenths of it already" (Bateson & Bateson, 1987, p. 173). Metaphorically, the "verites" lie "between the lines, and are re-constructed by the patterns that connect mind and nature" (pp. 156–58). However, Bateson (1979) did give way to the "manner of search . . . a method of *double* or *multiple* comparison," which is the *pattern that connects* in this study

> in which the combining of information of different sorts or from different sources results in something more than addition. The aggregate is

> greater than the sum of its parts because the combining of the parts is not a simple adding but is the nature of a multiplication or a fractionation, or the creation of a logical product. A momentary gleam of enlightenment.
>
> [p. 86]

This study of change of world view, of the science of cybernetic patterns of organization, of shock and dissonance, involved a like manner of meta-search of which Gregory Bateson wrote (1972, 1979, 1987). It involved what Bateson called "Learning Levels Zero to IV" (1972, p. 293). Learning *about* Learning II contraries or schismogenic double-binds involves patterns of dissonance; "gaps" and "loopholes" appear. One is additionally perturbed by epistolary of th-alk and dialogue of "that's the way it's always been and will remain" (p. 303) or "the things in life are just too complicated for me to understand." Even so, Bateson (1972) suggested that if

> the creature is driven to level III by the "contraries" generated at level II, then we may expect that it is the resolving of these contraries that will constitute positive reinforcement at level III. Such resolution can take many forms . . . some fall by the wayside . . . labeled psychotic. . . . Others . . . collapsing much that was learned at level II, [are] no longer in charge of organizing behavior . . . For others, more creative, the resolution of contraries reveals a world in which personal identity merges into all the process of relationship in some vast ecology or aesthetics of cosmic interactions.
>
> [p. 305]

Or the earlier inference by the author concerning the similarity and profound difference in the connotation and denotation of the key terms used in describing recursive patterns of feedback. The terms *complementary* and *complimentary* misconstrued or simply misspelled change context and meaning in a profound sense. The whole system explodes in directions mere mortals fear to tread; i.e., a *left-handed compliment* is insincere or dubious. And so, having passed "through the threat of that chaos where thought becomes impossible" (Bateson, 1979, p. 143), the "reward of change" of the Learning III journey, according to William Blake's poetic description, is:

> To see the Whole World in a Grain of Sand,
> And a Heaven in a Wild Flower,
> Hold Infinity in the palm of your hand,
> And Eternity in an hour. [cited in Bateson, 1972, p. 306]

Less poetically, but perhaps more practicable, Bredo at the November 1987 meeting of American Education Studies Association (AESA) presented his paper titled "Bateson's Communicative Approach to Learning" (1987), implying that if one were looking for research data suggesting Learning III, "one would look for accellerating (or decelleration) [sic] rates of learning" at Levels I and II. Learning II "modulates . . . either enhancing or interfering with" Learning III (p. 9). Bateson's (1972, 1979, 1987) Logical Levels of Learning change fit as new tricks of a cybernetic epistemology Keeney (1983) implied as "process of knowing maintaining and constructing a new world of experience" (p. 90). The task of imagining and increasing the stock of meta-models that depict personal "gleams of enlightenment" involves previously uncharted dangerous levels. What remains, then, is the "fit of the organism's internal demands for coherence, and . . . the external requirements of environment" (p. 144).

Bredo (1987), in the paper referred to in the previous paragraph, suggested "ways in which learning research is specific to a broader meta-context," using Bateson's approach to learning. He went on to imply:

> All of our studies of learning, as well as the behavior of the learners being studied, are informed by societal conceptions of what "knowledge" is and what it means to "learn," and what a "learner" or an "expert" is. In other words, there are broad social/historical contexts of learning research which limit our ability to generalize. Thinking about the concepts used in learning research itself, and the historical origins of these concepts, can help give one a sense of their recency and limits. [p. 11]

Bredo's November 1987 paper helped keep this author's study/inquiry under way, even though its embarkation date was almost a year before. That reinforcement was evidenced in/by the broad focus of this study. Just such limited knowledge of "broad social/historical contexts of learning . . . [and] historical origins if these concepts . . . " assuredly limits the "ability to generalize." Floating about with *Uncertainty Principle* is not without rewards. (Bredo must have heard the author's SOS.) Its final destination is not so far off course.

The final section, involving Student Factors—Cybernetic Shock, is the synthesis of responses from "shipmates" on this voyage of *Uncertainty Principle*. The data were taken from logged "becoming" interview dialogues involving graduate students and the author. Heuristic "un-methods" seek to illuminate the theme and formulate questions. In reporting of data, expressed verbal content (EVC) is intended to convey how students found "what *is,* as it *is*" (Douglass and Moustakas, 1985, pp. 35–55).

Interview/Dialogue Synthesis

> If you want to know how people feel: what they experience and what they remember, what their emotions and motives are like, and the reasons for acting as they do—why not ask them?
>
> (G. W. Allport, cited in Jahoda, Deutsch and Cook, p. 152 [1951])

At the heart of heuristic inquiry there is emphasis on "true intersubjectivity; . . disclosing the self as a way of facilitating disclosure from others. . . . When we know a thing from our own experience, its meaning can be recognized in others, without the typical accountings and explanations" (Douglass and Moustakas, 1985, p. 50). The open-ended interviews generally focused on graduate students' subjective-dependent (objective) (Maturana, cited in Segal, 1986) experience involved in being and/or becoming cybernetic epistemologists. (That is, from a cybernetic of cybernetic level the observer's observations may have included his/her act of observing.) The interviews took on the flavor of dialectic; all but one volunteer ($N=7$ of $n=67$) had completed course work and written and oral comprehensives for the attainment of the degree of doctor of philosophy (Ph.D.) in counseling education. The six were either entering or actively engaged in the process of dissertation. Scheduled interview questions (appendix C) generally focused on experienced higher learning processes:

Who or what helped you through this process?
What have been the ramifications involving your personal and professional life?
What is the impact on your family and friends?
What conclusions have you reached?

Punctuated patterns emerged. Keeney (1983) noted: "The most basic act of epistemology is to create a distinction . . . by distinguishing one pattern from another we are able to know our world . . . [this is] a major foundation of cybernetic thinking" [pp. 60–65).

Maturana's "Observer-Based Science" (cited in Segal, 1986) has developed "Operations of Distinction" for talking about patterns of experience referred to in this study/inquiry (p. 00). According to neurophilosopher Maturana, application of these operations of distinction may permit the claim that the study/inquiry may be valid in a community of observers. Maturana's operations are spelled out in the literature review section of "Cybernetics and Beyond," page 000. Generally heuristic inquiry does not require formal hypothetical statements as such; it represents what *is* as it *is*. (On the other hand, throughout this study/inquiry, the author has attempted the responsible use of various traditional/residual and emergent descriptive methods.) An application of Maturana's operations to the present study follows:

1 *Make a distinction:* Interviews/dialogue with a sample of graduate students that focused on the experience of change of world view (becoming a cybernetic epistemologist) may facilitate subjective (objective) (Maturana's observer-dependent) expression of content or verbalization (EVC) of patterns of intellectual, emotional, and psychological tension and discomfort (cognitive dissonance; Learning II). Further perturbations may elicit expression of verbal content (EVC) of patterned responses of confusion and concern or *cybernetic shock* involved at Learning Level III change—a cybernetic epistemology; the verbal content (EVC) of the experiences may be isomorphic to the patterns illustrated in the study, tracing patterns of change of world view.
2 *Construct hypotheses:* (A) Becoming a cybernetic epistemologist involves reports or the expression of verbal content (EVC) of patterned dissonance at L. II. Dissonance moves some toward cybernetic shock of L. III. (B) Becoming a cybernetic epistemologist does not involve reports or the expression of verbal content (EVC) of patterned dissonance or any movement toward cybernetic shock of L. III.
3 *Compute:* If experiential reports or verbal content (EVC) during focused interviews of the sample ($N=7$) match the researcher's description of experienced patterned dissonance, then further perturbation may effect reports or the expression of verbal content (EVC) of experienced *cybernetic shock* involved at Learning Level III change. Dissonance may then be concluded to be a necessary intervening (Kuhn's anomalous) variable involved in change of world view.
4 *Validate*: Heruistic interviews conducted by the researcher focused on *the patterns that connect* this composite unity of learning level changes, of a pattern of cognitive dissonance involved with being or becoming cybernetic epistemologists and *cybernetic shock.* Step #3 may validate the construct of step #2. The experiential accounts (EVC) of the sample ($N=7$) may be considered isomorphic to the patterned phenomenon described in the illustrations and text of this study/inquiry.

Maturana (cited in Segal, 1986) held: "Everything that is said is said by an observer to another observer who may be him or herself . . . it is always the observer who makes the distinctions . . . unities he specifies come into existence through the observer's operations of distinction" (pp. 60–65). More specifically, audiotape transcriptions (EVC) were distinguished, computed, validated, and synthesized according to the following;

Themes = Traditional (T), Residual (R), Emergent and Beyond (EB), conceptual frames of world view.
Categories = Intellectual response (IR); Emotional response (ER); Cognitive Dissonance or L. II (CD); Cybernetic Shock (CS) and cybernetic epistemology or L. III (CE).
Patterns: Linear (L); Circular (C); Shift (S); Recursive (rc); Triangular (tr) (and emergent patterns).
Subjective rating scale = of degree and/or intensity from 1 (low) to 10 (high) of dissonance/shock. For the overall rating of experienced learning change a Likert scale was used: extremely negative; negative; neutral; positive; extremely positive.

Generally interview/dialogues evolved alternating focused statements on interviewer/respondent common knowledge with open-ended perturbations and self-disclosure. Requests were made for subjective-dependent (objective) (EVC) understanding or definitions involved in self-reflective intellectual and emotional responses to dissonance, *cybernetic shock,* and cybernetic epistemology. Flexibility of perturbations/questions/probes/self-disclosure dictated the dialogues. Aggregate reporting of data synthesis evolved from the following statements and open-ended perturbations: (NOTE: *Subject headings were not referred to in a direct manner* until focused descriptive responses surfaced in interviews, i.e., experienced "psychological tension and/or discomfort" = cognitive dissonance; confusion and/or concern = cybernetic shock. The following question/statement list serves only as an outline to orient the reader and give a flavor of dialectic. Shared experience is a rich source of understanding phenomenon.) The following was not verbalized or effected in this exact format.

Cybernetic Epistemology

Focusing opening statement: " 'Understanding cybernetic epistemology may completely alter one's habits of actions' "—Keeney called it " 'the deepest order of change . . . ' " (1983, p. 6)
Questions: What is your definition of cybernetic epistemology?

How do you see yourself as being or becoming a cybernetic epistemologist?

Cognitive Dissonance

In any way did your introduction to a cybernetic epistemology constitute any psychological tension or discomfort, or lack of fit with a previous way of thinking?
Do you remember a theory of cognitive dissonance?
How do you recall or define cognitive dissonance?
Given your definitions, was there any fit of cognitive dissonance and the feelings you experienced when introduced to a cybernetic epistemology?
How would you label the prior cognitions with which cybernetic epistemology involved cognitive dissonance?
Statement of definitions of cognitive dissonance: Festinger (1957), cited in Reynolds (1971), defined it as " 'two or more cognitions that compete or conflict, that logically do not 'fit' " (p. 39).
On a scale from 1 to 10, with 1 as low and 10 as high, how would you rate the degree/intensity of cognitive dissonance?
Statement: Kuhn (1962, 1970) called this an "acute personal crisis . . . experienced as disorientation . . . a revolutionary change of world view" (p. 112).
What were your feelings?
What means did you and/or others use to reduce or resolve cognitive dissonance?
What were the ramifications of cognitive dissonance?
In what ways did knowing cybernetic epistemology affect your cognitive dissonance?
Was there any confusion and concern involved with the complexity of cybernetic epistemology?

Cybernetic Shock

Statement or definition of cybernetic shock—the confusion and concern involved in resolution/reduction of cognitive dissonance or resolving the eternal contraries of either/or double-binds . . . the higher level of learning change Bateson called Learning III change.
How did the new epistemology fit your personal and professional life?
Describe your initial response to knowing cybernetic epistemology.

Was it anything like Toffler's (1970) *Future Shock?* Psychological or physiological shock?
How would you rate cybernetic shock on a scale from 1 to 10?
Is there any evidence suggesting becoming a cybernetic epistemologist is like becoming a non-conformist?
Initially, did your change of world view involve any feeling akin to alienation? From yourself? Others? The world?
Are there any others—other than peers or faculty members—you know who seem to know cybernetic epistemology?
What are your future plans for the use of your "new" cybernetic epistemology? Is it practicable? Can its use be sustained?
Can it be integrated in your world?
Given the learning experience of becoming a cybernetic epistemologist, the cognitive dissonance, and cybernetic shock, what is your overall rating of that experience? Extremely Positive, Positive, Neutral, Negative, Extremely Negative? Or again, on a scale of 1 to 10 . . .
What conclusions have you reached?

Demographics (Respondent = *R*)

Age: Range 31 to 44; mean 36; mode 33.
Gender: $N=7$ or 5F and 2*M* ($n=67$ - 2: 1 *F: M*)
Undergraduate majors: speech pathology/audiology, biology, education, history, nursing, philosophy, and psychology.
Master's level: audiology, education, nursing; experimental psychology, clinical psychology, counseling psychology, and social work.
Religious preference: "Don't know; I was raised Protestant. I'm Protestant—I believe in God."
"Was Catholic—although today it's no preference."
"Well, I come closest to Buddhist in that sense . . . (raised Irish Catholic)."
"Protestant—whatever that is."
"Agnostic."
"None. My background is Baptist, but I never really led an active church role at all."
"Protestant, I was raised Protestant. My father was Jewish. I think my father's different background again has exposed me to diversity."
Marital status: Single, never married (1); married without children (1); married with children (3); divorced/remarried with children (1); divorced with children (1).

Children: 9 Total; mode 2. Age: range 1 to 17 years.
Professional status: counseling intern, counselor, nurse, clinical nurse specialist, clinical psychologist (part-time), psychotherapist (part-time), social worker, college teacher (full- and part-time).
When did you take Advanced Individual, Marriage, and Family Therapy (ED 145-665)?: 1982 (audited '85), '83, '84, '86, '87.
Who was your professor?: Ray/Dorothy Becvar.
Finally: *When was dissonance/shock at its highest intensity?* At the start of the program? With a particular course/professor? With the advanced course? Studying for "Comps?" Dissertation process?:
R's: First classes ("non-understanding of readings and language of cybernetic 'jargon' " of Keeney [1983], and Bateson [1972, 1979].) ($N=5$).
R's: Advanced Individual, Marriage and Family Development & Therapy ("misnomer—a philosophy course.") ($N=4$).
R's: Dissertation process ("contradiction to learning change") ($N=4$).
R's: Study for comprehensives ("chance to pull it all together") ($N=5$). However, "comps" themselves another "contradiction" in learning change. ($N=6$).

Theme

(Reporting in aggregates, Respondent = *R*.)
Theme: Being or becoming a cybernetic epistemologist:
R #1 shared: "I guess I don't consider myself one . . . I really am uncomfortable with that. . . . It's so linear to put a label on something. . . . I guess I would say that sometimes I seem to perceive and understand things in a cybernetic pattern—with a circular understanding."
Another R (#3) shared: "If the fanaticism of my studies is an indication of being a cybernetic epistemologist and I guess that's true because I really enjoy doing it."
Five R's considered themselves as becoming:
R #4: "Still developing—I think it's a process of becoming—I haven't completed the process."
R #2: "I think definitely becoming. I think that I intellectually made the transition—but I emotionally behaviorally catch myself doing things in the old way—meaning before the graduate experience. I'm still becoming."
R #5: "Oh, I think definitely in the process . . . I'm not sure whether anyone ever really gets to that point in the purest sense."
R #6: "As a matter of fact, I do see it as an ongoing process. Yet, when you examine it closely enough, at least for me, my conclusion was that

you know, I've always been becoming one, I just didn't know it . . . the trick is to know it."
R #7: "I think it's always . . . I think I am a cybernetic epistemologist, and I am becoming one. I think I certainly am becoming as well as already using some of it."

Theme: Traditional world view understanding R's shared were: "Cause and effect—absolute reality—A causes B . . . "
"I think probably the majority of society has much more absolutistic views, believing that there is a true reality that everybody experiences the same way is true . . . thinking that there was absolute truth one way of looking at the world."
"Regimented, rigid, inflexible, one-way . . . "
"[World] in terms of dynamics and energy and transfer of force—that kind of view—mechanistic traditional epistemology . . . were taken to be ultimate reality."
"World view, i.e., personality, the more traditional ways of defining personality—because it gets into right or wrong or good or bad."
"It's sort of like a metaphysics that isn't aware of itself. So really essentially I think it was a Cartesian or Newtonian kind of world view—very much cause and effect and very linear things."
"Our traditional ways of thinking about events or people are not really all that inclusive. . . . Simple cause and effect, and I think things become much more ambiguous. You can't say this is right, this is wrong, this is black, this is white."

Theme: Residual "Revolutions as Changes of World View" (Kuhn, 1962, 1970, pp. 111–35) were "shift" or "simple circular cybernetics":
R #1 shared personal and professional instances of "tremendous conflict" referred to as rooted in: "being in a different philosophy. . . . My [spouse] is really big on the old way of thinking; we get into minor arguments whenever I bring up the matter of perception and [her/his] way of seeing it—[s/he] gets exasperated—increased when I was in graduate school—it's decreased now." Professional instances of conflict management this *R* shared: "confrontation, walking away, or living with it—unless it's important enough—if I make a major thing out of everything . . . whether or not I want to be hurt, or shunned, laughed at or ridiculed . . . "
R #2, in reference to "shift" of world views, offered, "I'll tell you it has been traumatic—it has been absolutely traumatic—it's been painful, it's been uncomfortable—it's been discombobulating . . . for the first 2 years I didn't know what the hell was going on!"

R #3, on "crisis": "It creates crisis to solve that problem . . . but I am in enormous crisis right now. I don't like going home, being depressed all the time. [Described ongoing professional "power struggle" and "negative coalitions" involved.] I've never been in crisis for so long as this was over the last few years."
R #4 related: "Taking time . . . that allows me to shift from one role to another . . . I talk in cycles of behavior . . . circular thinking and systems type thinking . . . spirals. That's how I think a lot now. I guess in my mind's eye I see cybernetic as a spiral, a pattern, a process that is more circular, okay?"
R #6: "Maybe the best description of what I experienced relative to the program, would be like a religious conversion experience . . . as an analogy—not in a literal sense."
R #7: "Kuhn was really about how our epistemology and I think he calls it a paradigm, impacts how we foresee reality."

Theme: Emergent and beyond theoretical concepts:
R #1 shared that "structure determinism—the whole biological theory and phenomenon—Maturana has really allowed me to pull things together . . . I go more to the traditional biology that helps me put things together—I think we need both (philosophy & biology) I don't understand to the level that you do philosophy."
R #2, after finding him/herself caught up in an actual philosophical meta–double-bind in the dialogue over the concepts of self versus constructivism, was perturbed to seek resolution outside the frame of a paradoxical either/or "Game Without End." "Yes, it's going out of the perimeter what we're doing now—we have this idea—I LOVE THAT!—the solution—yes, this was a tremendous realization for me! Something that has been rattling me—either/or—why not both? AND! Why must you choose?"[See *cybernetic shock* R #2, pages 000–000, for "root" [EVC] reference to this conceptual resolution of a meta double-bind.]
R #3 also described: "I consider myself a radical now, you know, I have grown in my mind. This foolish concept of the 'self' at all—it doesn't matter—high self-esteem or low self-esteem, it's believing in your "SELF" in the first place. I'm not trying to keep up with psychology any more. I'm telling you the real dirt. I don't tell anyone else . . . people come in to me with 'problems' I don't think are problems, because someone has so formulated them." This *R* went on to share, "In my 20's I did all this meditating. Well I started again. . . . This is an opportunity for second order and third order learning. If I work here [professionally] in this state of crisis, something's got to give, there

will be some reorganization. I mean you're looking for new experiences. That's the most powerful recent one I had. You know I hate it here [job], but in a sense I love it because this has been a challenge for me. . . . I'm going to figure out how to deal with this system."

R #4 related an understanding of "the constructivists' view that we all construct our own reality. I think we construct our emotional response . . . we construct a lot more than that. I think we construct cause and effect in many ways, be it circular . . . we have different descriptions . . . based on our general epistemology. But I also don't believe there's two distinct epistemologies. I also don't believe there's two distinct epistemologies to lock in view. I think there's a lot . . . the old Lockean view, either/or, I guess I think the majority of people probably hold not that exact epistemology but much of that. But I just don't think it's either/or. Yeah, I'm a *pessimistic* world viewer. I know loads of people who are just as *optimistic* as they come, they believe in an absolute right and wrong, reality is an absolute, but they are not the least bit pessimistic."

R #3: "From my viewpoint [cybernetic epistemology] if you don't see it as a way of thinking—you know, you can use and go through the books, I mean whether it's a paradoxical therapy book or a resistance to change book where they offer strategies, tactics or whatever, tactics of change, that if you don't . . . if it isn't a way of thinking as opposed to a way of doing therapy, then what you're going to find is first order of change as opposed to second order of change. . . . "

R #6: "I've been particularly influenced by the constructivism epistemology that's come out of this. If you immerse yourself in the assumptions associated with that epistemology of constructivism, I think it's a real shocker. It really is!"

Categories

Category—Cognitive dissonance of L. II, the "psychological tension and discomfort" of "paradoxical contraries and double-binds" that drive some to cybernetic epistemology and *cybernetic shock* of L. III. Cognitive dissonant probes for *Rs* definitions were generally consonant with the study and Festinger's (1957) concept:

R #1: "Lack of fit—a discord—doesn't feel harmonious. Cognitive dissonance is when you believe something and your actions don't support your belief and you become less in conflict with yourself by bringing the two together—change belief or actions." Later, the same *R* shared, "Dissonance has a negative connotation to me. I don't find it [cybernetic epistemology] dissonant as not congruent." Further into the dialogue s/he, in relating a case description, said, "I felt more dissonance and conflict over this case getting different points of view from all different people . . . cognitive dissonance? Oh, cognitive dissonance a '9,' still a '6' talking about it today." This *R* described being "relieved me within myself" by consulting with a professor whose suggested intervention fit that of "therapeutic triangulation."

R # (see pp. 110 and 115–116) described experiences correlating with the hypothesized cognitive dissonant feelings as "overwhelming; tearing my hair out; shook my world view—to doubt everything . . . ," s/he gave the following definition of cognitive dissonance: "As I remember it it's when . . . my definition would be—I guess when there's a discrepancy between how you behave and how you think and this creates a state of tension—behavior is very public—you think one way or believe one way—but your behavior is public . . . so overt—it's hard to deny when you've done something. What you do is change in order to diminish the dissonance. Change the belief in the direction of the behavior." This *R* gave the example of "having an abortion—if prolife." S/he went on, "Possible to have a state of intrapsychic tension so what I might do is to diminish—change my beliefs. Certainly there's tension—no doubt about that—it's now becoming more exciting—not quite so painful. Yeah, you know I never thought about that—but that's a *Very Good Metaphor* [cognitive dissonance] for what's happened . . . it fits my definition perfectly. . . . I like your metaphor of dissonance. Oh, and that comes from psychology for goodness sake . . . like Ellis' 'should's'—everybody 'SHOULD' see the world—and they don't—and that's the dissonance!" This same *R* rated cognitive dissonance "at times a '10' or above for at least two years. It just turned me upside-down!" Again, another professor and meaningful dialogue with peers are the means for reduction of cognitive dissonance—however, this *R* shared a personally meaningful quotation of Varela's: " 'There is alienation in liberation,' my god that's so true. . . ."

R #6 remembered cognitive dissonance this way: "My practical working definition of it now as opposed to an academic definition is just that we behave now and explain it to ourselves later. And we kind of—you know, our behavior precedes our ideas about our behavior. And we really don't know ourselves and we use our contexts to explain whatever it is we do. We confuse the order of those two things. That understanding of what we do made us do what we do when its the other way around." This *R* talked around a self-rating of cognitive dissonance, but gave close to fifteen examples that infer that cognitive dissonance was/is driving her/him to higher learning levels of change. Reduction and partial resolution of cognitive dissonance is sought in deep Eastern meditative practices that "was my lifeboat before . . . I got this practice out of mothballs and began again, and well—how do you understand what's happening? You know, if things are getting better."

R #4 described a definition of cognitive dissonance, calling it: "Clearly non-understanding. A disequilibrium, discomfort. I mean all of those were there. There's a discomfort, because it doesn't fit—and I need to do some mental gymnastics. So there's a certain tension, a certain unbalance, and then eventually there's some adjustments that are made in the whole system and it seems to fit and the system has grown in the process—because now it encompasses . . . yeah, its grown more 'complex.' I really don't like the word 'shift' [either]. To me shift implies moving from this to this. Linear, okay again. . . . I see it as a broadening so that there are now more possibilities. The Piagetian model [adaptation] and disequilibrium to me is kind of a form of dissonance where things don't seem to fit. So there's some discomfort because it doesn't fit, it doesn't seem to work together. I think we all experience a lot of cognitive dissonance at various times and it can be on tiny little things that are just a fact." Later, cognitive dissonance was self-rated by this *R* as equal to "maybe a '4' . . . disequilibrium was higher—any time I read Keeney or Bateson . . . it wasn't very long or deep." Resolution or reduction is seen as achieved in daily half-hour drives to and from work/home, "either a meditation, a thinking time, I'll sing with the music . . . a shifting of gears time . . . allows me to shift from one role to the other." S/he remarked, "I've got so many things to deal with that I can't luxuriate in mental cognitive, I don't want to say "games" because that implies something—it's just, I don't have time to have a long or deep disequilibrium. . . ."

R #5: "That things that you had thought or believed before, that something has come along that has caused a shake-up in that or maybe has caused you to question or . . . how would I say it? [Cognitive dissonance] basically [is] 'caused' discomfort. What happens is you try to find something or some way of either resolving it or getting it to go away—or get rid of it. . . . Cognitive dissonance, I would say probably at least an '8' and it lasted for 4 years. And I still struggle with it." Cognitive dissonance for the dissertation process increased: "Hell yes. I'd say a '10.' Because I don't . . . I think that rather than it being a positive learning experience and something that is useful, that it becomes a chore, an almost insurmountable task, that you get to the point where . . . that it becomes product oriented as opposed to quality and a real contribution. Part of it is that I think that this [dissertation] process in some ways is contradictory to what we've learned. I think it's a real contradiction. *It's either/or!*"

R #6: (Cognitive dissonance) "I think for me it comes down to experiencing contradictions, whether it be in terms of a contradiction between what you're thinking, believing and acting, or a contradiction in beliefs. For me, I think both apply but I think there was more of a contradiction between different assumptions. . . . You know, I think you have to have that kind of contradiction to drive . . . not negative, I would equate it with like a creative turmoil—just a tension—a creative kind of thing, and I think to grow it's what has to happen. It's disequilibrium. I would say it was pretty intense, I would say around '9,' even '10' for me." This *R* described talks with a professor and his/her spouse who's "been very supportive of me . . . we don't sit down and discuss these kinds of things in the manner that you and I are discussing them now . . . [she/he's] very bright . . . really not that academically inclined . . . been there when I needed . . . especially when I went through that crisis, that dissonance, at its acute point. I felt depressed for a while, really down trying to think it out—cognitive dissonance is apropos. . . ."

R #7: "I guess the piece of it that I use is . . . somehow—there needs to be some, there's really a strong relationship and there has to be some fit, a connection that people make between their behaviors and their belief systems about these behaviors and how they value these behaviors . . . let's say if I buy something and spend a lot of money for it, I have to value it highly . . . value is not in the object itself. There has to be some fit." Cognitive dissonance was rated as a " '5,' initially that first class . . . 9 or 10 months later it was very low ('1' or '2')."

Categories—cybernetic epistemology or shock of L. III. An understanding/definition of cybernetic epistemology and the "confusion and concern" of cybernetic shock at L. III is expressed as whole—reinforcing the composite unity or cognitive-body of the study/inquiry:

R #1: Cybernetic epistemology: "It's process—not necessarily cybernetic epistemology but a systems thinking. Cybernetic epistemology—thinking in systems." Cybernetic shock: "Confusion and concern? Oh, sure—or sure like the first time I was talking with [professor]—about [medical patients'] cases. Who tried to convince me it was just a relationship problem and something in these families—like schizophrenic families. NO WAY did I believe that and it caused a tremendouos confusion and concern—I'm sorry I couldn't imagine how one could possibly believe that—and I hope today s/he doesn't believe that—because I really think we need both. I think many things fit systems theory—and rejecting them makes me crazy. Finding them makes me happy. . . . Structure determinism the whole biological theory and phenomenon—Maturana has really allowed me to pull things together."

R #1 self-rated the overall experience of becoming a cybernetic epistemologist as: "Still developing—a positive '7.' I retook the philosophical course—I had to learn all that stuff at the last minute—the year prior to taking exams." Cognitive dissonance and cybernetic shock was at its highest studying for comprehensive exams. Not dissonance or shock but "depression" was the descriptive term shared for the dissertation process.

Cybernetic epistemology was understood by another R (#2) as: "Attending to process, context, respecting and seeing the validity of everybody's perception of the world. . . . A constructed view of the world—there's validity in everybody's perception—[we] pull things out—that support the world view that we have—recognize that there are things we miss that we choose not to attend to that others might—which amounts to the difference in behaviors and the way of thinking—ways of looking at the world. The constructed world view, the ongoing process of always being constructed, always being modified . . . Attention to context, attending to where, when, or how behavior was occurring—if inconsistent I go with behavior and context; would this behavior be different in a different setting—a tremendous leap for me!"

Cybernetic shock was evidenced in dialogue with this *R* (#2; see p. 112) as s/he reflected on the author's metaphor of *cybernetic shock,* studying constructivism while studying for comprehensives: "I began to feel alone—it was a crisis of alienation—feeling detached from my family, feeling detached from my friends, and I couldn't—I can't even verbalize it—they didn't think the way that I did—that it was my beliefs that were changing—and I was leaving what was comfortable, but what was really no longer compatible—because I saw something bigger and better that I could operate from—it's so true—having trouble finding words for this—the alienation—the loneliness that comes with liberation. I felt so lonely the last couple of years. Even knowing intellectually that there are colleagues of mine who have experienced much the same things. I just felt like that—I'm all that I've got—that's what's so frightening. But in order to get there—one had to realize that maybe there is no common way—there is no common belief. Unless, of course you choose that; but that there may not be anybody who thinks exactly like you. We all construct our reality—and in that sense we're alone? In that sense—talk about existential anxiety! Confusion in thinking—but then if everybody's view of the world is valid—think of all the billions of people—then, what makes me worthwhile? What makes me unique or different? How can I stand out? How can I make my belief and my behavior and my existence meaningful to me—if now—*I think I'm running into a double-bind here!* Because if everybody thought the same maybe it would be easier to make a mark. But now everybody is allowed or I'm allowing them to have their own perceptions their own existence—so how do I—if that in itself is different about all of us—I'm on to something but I can't quite verbalize it. If everybody is different in the fact that they construct their own reality—then how do I make myself stand out? How do I make my existence—I mean if this is the run of constructivism—in sense I'm a conformist—because I recognize everybody has got their own beliefs—even though it's different—I'm a conformist! *This isn't making any sense! I'm getting caught up in a double-bind. . . ."* (This *R's* description is of being driven to L. III, for resolution of dissonance at L. II see page 110, R#2). This *R* (#2) went on to rate the overall experience as "a 'ten,' beneficial—no pain, no gain." Dissonance/shock was at its highest "at first with Human Ecology Development, then Social Ecology."

R #3 on cybernetic epistemology: I hesitate because it would be hard to answer in a sentence or less, but . . . well, the first thing I want to take is the word epistemology . . . and for me that is the level of cognitive organization one above the level of conceptualizations and kind of the rules for generating concepts. Cybernetic epistemology to me would indicate a set of rules for generating concepts that, you know, will organize the world in terms of an information flow. I have to contrast [it with] physicalistic epistemology . . . this cybernetic stuff is an expression of what I've been thinking all along. . . . Desire creates suffering in the world. And there's no need to solve problems if you didn't assume that you had them in the first place. It's very Eastern; it was almost a complete restatement of that. I could actually study a system I agree with—a relief. I love this stuff. I really do. . . . You can let your commitment to a system of thinking blind you to all other ways of thinking. To be a good cybernetic epistemologist to me, you need to always be questioning whether this is the way you should be thinking. You should always have double descriptions going on—[or] you've reified the word. I still really question cybernetics too through my education. I don't want to become a true believer and never question the foundations I stand on. I don't want to get premature hardening of the categories."

Cybernetic shock involved, for this R (#3), was "much older than most. It was like someone pulled the rug out from under me." This *R* shared intimate feelings encountering double-binds involved in professional life: "In a social context where no one else really subscribes to systems theory . . . my first raise was postponed because my reports didn't reflect the belief that alcoholism is a disease . . . quite a crisis . . . it wasn't a personal thing, but a socially induced crisis. . . . I left [that position]. . . . I'll tell you what new double-bind that created for me [in a different setting]. I was considered something like a heretic . . . I was being socially ostracized and I was patronized and treated as a very dumb person . . . whatever I said would be ignored. . . . I sensed this was a dangerous environment to talk about drinking anymore . . . I was in trouble and I knew it. A Cold War, I held on for about a year trying to fit in somehow . . . not talking about drinking. I was raised and Irish Catholic kid and whenever something's wrong, you think you did something. That you deserve the guilt somehow, that you're responsible. This was a fault back in my older epistemology and I constantly backslide into that kind of thinking of feeling guilty and responsible. . . . I got here and I got treated like hell. It was really horrible. I came home and I wept every night. I mean, it was horrible . . . it was just plain loneliness on my part—a fate worse than death—you'll do anything to fit it. In my heart I admit to myself that really reading Bateson and Keeney and trying to impress them was not the solution, but if anything maintained the problem. . . . That went on for months and months—there was a lot of depression at that time. . . . The smarter I got the worse it got . . . symmetrical escalation . . . one-up-manship. . . . Also, what I learned from this experience that I get working with . . . is that what happens when you're committed to a perspective and for the life of you you can't figure out how to use it to get yourself out of hot water . . . you keep trying all these different solutions and making sure one is different from the last one because you read that in the MRI (Mental Research Institute) approach. And that doesn't seem to work and then finally for me it was saying, it was just assuming that I needed to solve anything . . . just relax . . . don't worry and do the best you can. . . ." This extremely articulate *R* rated the overall experience of cognitive dissonance/cybernetic shock/cybernetic epistemology as: "Probably a '10'; I'm very boorish on the whole!"

The next R #4: "Cybernetic epistemology? I couldn't really define cybernetic epistemology. I can define, I think, epistemology and I can define cybernetic, but together, I'm not sure I have a definition. To me epistemology is a process, a kind of way of knowing something, a way of understanding, a way of perceiving. That's pretty clear to me. Cybernetic is a little bit more technical, more tricky. And I guess in my mind's eye I see cybernetic as a spiral, a pattern, a process that is more circular, okay? . . . just a complex intertwining of things. But, I don't see cybernetic epistemology as a thing. It's kind of way of knowing that involves these complex circles, patterns, spirals, etc. . . . I don't see it as a single entity. . . I don't see it on top of other ways of knowing . . . kind of a different way of knowing that sometimes I'm functioning under that umbrella and sometimes I'm not. I seem to flip in and out. I seem to be in both sometimes. I seem to be in multiple." The same *R* (#4) on *cybernetic shock,* "Well certainly there's some confusion. Probably, clearly life and living and everything that goes along with it is extremely complex in my view. And I just . . . I choose not to live at that level of complexity much of the time. . . . I don't deny that it's complex. I don't forget that it's complex. I just choose at times a more simpler way of interacting. It's not that it's not still confusing, it's kind of like on a back burner. I guess I can't relate to the word 'shock.' I don't see it so much as negative, I see it as too dramatic and I guess the term *shock* as I understand it and its many definitions just doesn't fit what I experienced. . . . *Shock* for me is too dramatic a term to describe anything that I've experienced in this realm. . . . I just don't see it as a massive thing or a *shock* or an overwhelming type thing. I don't think *shock*. Clearly confusion. Clearly non-understanding, disequilibrium, discomfort. I mean all of those were there. . . . In some ways I felt alone and in some ways I didn't. . . . I guess one of the frustrating things was, in the past, before this doctoral program, my education has been full-time . . . I could really delve into it and feel myself—good word: 'immersed' in the process . . . so this has been different for me because I couldn't do that . . . [full-time] I probably ate and thought 'student-ese' a lot more than I can in the doctoral program." This *R* (#4) consistently nullified the term *shock*. When probed for an overall self-rating: "I never said I had 'shock.' *Dissonance* yes. When was it most intense? Clearly the first course when I was first introduced to Keeney. Clearly in Human Development Ecology where we did Keeney and Bateson, some of the other people again, where the professor was very consistently talking cybernetic terminology throughout the course, and then of course in the *Advanced* course. . . . I don't see that as a negative aspect; I guess I just disagree with Keeney. . . . I think inevitably, though, it has effected many things that I'm probably not even aware of—most of it has to do with any level or human interaction. And human interaction can include me to me, within me. . . . During study for 'comps' my dissonance was called stress and panic, but wasn't so much of a cognitive, conceptual type thing—in some respects it was just the opposite—a wonderful time to integrate and work it together, so I would say dissonance over this epistemological type—epistemological dissonance was at a low. Stress was at a high. . . . I've had a lot of stress over the dissertation and I've had a lot of . . . some conceptual disagreements or concerns . . . either don't view things the way I do or don't understand them the way I do . . . it's not at all related to, or at least I don't perceive it as being related to cybernetic epistemology. For me it's more of a disagreement in terms of what is viable. . . ." S/he ended with, "So that's where my dissonance is coming, but it doesn't really have anything to do with cybernetic epistemology."

R #5 on cybernetic epistemology, "Things that occur, and particularly in regards to interactions between people . . . in order for behavior to occur or maintain itself, that it has to have a logical complement . . . the recursive pattern that if one is nagging—the nagger and the nagged and it just keeps up. One behavior is influenced by another. . . . Epistemology? A way of thinking, a way of doing things, a way of conceptualizing things. . . . To me epistemology is encompassing . . . it's your world view or how you put things together, the way you see people and the way you put that into practice."

R #5 *cybernetic shock,* "My biggest confusion and concern came in probably realizing that you are in the minority when you think this way . . . [cybernetic epistemology]. Yeah, I see it as non-conformist. Well, it's not in the mainstream of thinking. But who wants to be like everybody else? . . . I was in the closet with it. Basically this has helped me to accept that that's the way I am, that's the way I think and there's not a damn thing wrong with it. . . . As a matter of fact, now I am more at peace with myself and more content than I've ever been in my life . . . it has been a way of getting more in touch with myself, causing me to examine and explore not only myself but my world, and its caused me to look at everything differently." This *R* self-rated cybernetic shock as a "real high '5.' "

R #6: "Cybernetic epistemology involves looking for patterns. To use Bateson's well quoted phrase, *patterns that connect,* yet that's metaphysical. I think that I see cybernetic epistemology as a kind of metatheory; meta in the sense that it's really integrated a lot of constructs and concepts at different levels . . . really difficult to translate that into pragmatic terms. Maybe I'm still struggling with that . . . honestly at this point some things are still *fuzzy* . . . still formulating some things and I really haven't quite landed . . . still up in the air in some ways . . . I don't see that as being bad at all. I would call it a kind of creative turmoil. And I would think that if anybody who goes through this kind of program and they allow themselves to be affected by it, then I would think that they would share some of the feelings I'm experiencing."

R #6 on cybernetic shock: "I think there is an emotional component with whatever assumption or belief one might have in a cognitive sense. I would say when that all hit me at once, you know, I would give it a '9.' I think it was the *Advanced Marriage and Family Therapy*

course that put it together for me, and then I came out of that feeling as if the world had been pulled out from underneath me and my universe changed! Yeah, my universe really changed!"
R #7's knowledge of cybernetic epistemology: "In some ways you know, it was almost a relief for me when I started sensing that *third level* of cybernetic epistemology because it is a solution, it's not a problem solving linear solution, but it's *higher level* solution in that I don't have to succumb to the either/or, I don't have to be a part of the duality, so it was a relief, that shift, it was great. . . . It's a paradox [L.II]. You can move beyond it. You can do something else. I love when . . . I think on a larger philosophical level too, to not have to be stymied, stuck, caught in paradox of life, but be able to take in the paradox and move on. . . ." [to L. III]
Cybernetic shock for R #7 was: " '2' maybe . . . I think that there's a concept at some level of that familiarity to me and that it wasn't shock. . . . I remember a childhood experience and I remember it very, very clearly. I used to lay out in the yard in the summertime and I would practice closing one eye and looking out at the sky and the grass and the trees, and then I would close the other eye and look at the sky and the grass and the trees. And they looked different colors depending on what eye I looked out of. And it had to do with I'm sure the light infraction or something. But over and over again I would do this and I would think now which one is the *real* way that it looks. And there wasn't any easy question in my dilemma. What color was it really? Because it was still a different color if I looked with both eyes" (binocular vision). *R #7* shared: "But there was a jolt at the beginning of the program because the whole way of talking, thinking and dealing with things was different than my psychology background . . . it just threw me for a loop."

Patterns That Connect

All five patterns specified, linear (L), simple circular (C), shifts (S), recursion (rc), and triangular (tr) (both therapeutic and pathological arrangements) plus two emergent patterns of dyads (D) or "negative coalitions" and spirals (sp) (possibly inferring intense escalating circular patterns) were mentioned throughout the dialogues.
R #1: "I don't always think about recursion—reciprocal effects . . . I'm approaching that. Old habit and pattern—old habits are hard to break." On *triangulation:* "A professor immediately drew a picture of triangulation, Mom and Grandma together—peace or split . . . with the kid

in the middle, that felt really, really good, that happened, truly a happy kid. . . ."

R #2 on linear: " . . . people had an impact on me—I had very little impact on them. . . . Psychiatry—a linear model. . . . Perhaps I was so locked into my linear view of the world . . . never did much critical thinking until the program at SLU . . . [linear] tunnel vision. I don't see myself ever going back to a linear way of thinking . . . except for one brief intervention with clients or like the 'flat earth hypothesis'—to build a tennis court!"

Circular: "I'm trying to move more into the middle—where it will be circular I guess. . . ." *Shift:* "It certainly felt like a shift—I think that was what was so painful! Using the Kuhnian metaphor the 'CRISIS' was really—all of the evidence building up on me—I could see—but I was fighting it—I was resisting it much like people do. . . ." *Recursion:* "feel caught in the middle . . . That you can't be a victim without being willing to assume that role. Recursion—reciprocity, 'A' does this to [me]—I didn't see myself as having impact on other people. . . . Systems related closer to bio-medical. . . . Keeney so hard to understand [cybernetic epistemology]—Kuhn gave some concrete—yeah, there was a shift from Newtonian to Einsteinian theory of relativity. Whereas Keeney—I have skimmed that book—six or seven times then still get something from it. . . ." *Triangular:* "that not being passive meant you didn't have to be aggressive—out of the frame or meta is assertive!"

R #3 shared, on linear concepts: "I majored in psychology at "X" [out-of-state] College and we had learned the behavioral perspectives and I remember constantly fighting that in my mind—coming out of that program with the assumption that I would always disagree with whatever I had to learn . . . put up with it in order to get to do what I wanted to do."

The same R (#3) on shift, dyads, recursion, and triangular patterns: "What made this such a horrible crisis in my mind in the systems trained person, one person can't be a problem. Everybody is the problem. . . . I have to believe that there's something I'm doing too that's creating that problem. . . . People who worked there before me said that it was just horrible before you were here, and it was still horrible. It was horrible afterwards. There had been four people, and two [negative] coalitions against each other before and the two had been defined as higher ranks in the personnel system and the other two—so these coalitions always fought it out. What it turned into when I came, I didn't try that hard to enlist another person, so it turned into like three against one—and I was kind of the one" (pathological triangulation).

With R #4: Linear was mentioned first as " 'vs. circular.' I don't see it as either linear or circular. I see it as if there are many, many different ways of knowing or perceiving and that through education I'm constantly adding to those. Some of them being bigger *shifts* than others . . . it's so linear to put a label on something or to say that somebody is a thing. . . I was introduced to a very simple view of family systems [out of state]. It's hard to explain. It's kind of a linear view of systems."

Circular and spiral with this R: "I guess I would say that sometimes I seem to perceive things in a—perceive and understand things in a cybernetic pattern—with a circular understanding. . . . When I'm with [clients] the spirals and circles are spinning in my brain—clearly with the families I work with I'm constantly aware of patterns and interactions and circularity . . . [cybernetic epistemology] as I think about it right now, it's probably more on the front burner than I realize because I've just accepted it as part of me now. And probably I'm not aware of how much I really do use the patterns and the circular . . . yeah, in terms of my thinking—by not being aware of it, I probably have just integrated it into other patterns."

R #5 on recursion: "The recursive pattern, where I guess you could say rather than one causes the other that one behavior begets another . . . it's a pattern that continues rather than being broken . . . there isn't a breaking point of you know, you did this—well I'm going to do this because after doing this then it gets back around to doing this again." This *R* shared an interesting metaphor of patterns that connect: "studying for 'comps' . . . it was like looking at it in the 'whole' rather than bits and pieces—it was like *weaving a pattern* . . . it was like it all started fitting together . . . it made sense . . . the first time that I had ever really sat down with other people and talked about it, explored it together, had gotten feedback, and in a sense it was like, you know, knowing that something wasn't comfortable anymore—that something didn't fit—and then it's like you know when talking with other people, it was like a validation to me that this jump that I had made or was in the process of making wasn't so crazy after all!"

On shift (R #5): "Through this process . . . maybe I have been able to make the shift from not thinking so much in the way that I had previously felt was expected of me, but that it has allowed me to do my own thinking."

R #6 on recursion: "Yet, at the same time, and drawing on recursion it's had its painfulness—part of growth. I'm going to invent my own universe I think—just kidding . . . I plan to continue to immerse myself in the literature. . . . I was looking for some kind of practical application . . . it dawned on me at some point that hey, it doesn't tell you *how* to do things really."

R #7 on patterns shared: "You know you jump levels. I think my overall understanding is at that [cybernetic epistemological] level, or what I strive for at that level, but it's like operationalizing . . . and the way I live my life, you know, I live my life in a linear way. Most things work in a linear way. At times I will stop and jump back and reflect and then it's very interesting to look at it in more of a cybernetic view. But I don't feel like I stay there."

Synthesis of Categories, Themes, and Patterned Responses

The challenge of the realization phase of heuristic inquiry is to let grow and mature processes and values that generate patterns of organization of a new reality, consistent with their true nature. The subjective-dependent (objective) verbal content (EVC) of respondents engaged in dialectic forms a network of strong support for the "Operations of Distinction" (Maturana, cited in Segal, 1987, p. 60; see pp. 103–4 and p. 62 of this study) hypothesis: Becoming a cybernetic epistemologist involves reports or the expression of verbal content of patterned dissonance of Learning Level II. Dissonance drives some to cybernetic shock at L. III.

Generally, expressed verbal content of intellectual and emotional responses provided strong support for the various references in the review of the literature. The study's face validity was enhanced by the sample interviewed. The focus of interview questions revealed heuristically the verbalization of content of intellectual and emotional responses of graduate students' introduction to cybernetic epistemology in the major area of Individual, Marriage and Family Development and Therapy of the Department of Counseling Education at St. Louis University. That synthesis follows. (Note: Expressed Verbal Content = EVC.)

How have you experienced this process?

Qualitatively the overall experiential process was valued as *extremely positive* (EVC). Degree/intensity of dissonance were reported ranging from a low of 4 to a high of 10; mode = 10; mean = 8. Duration of dissonance ranged from reports of "a very short time" to those of nine months to five years. Cybernetic shock for $N = 5$ ranged from 2 to 10; mode of 10; mean of 7.5. High dissonance correlated positively with shock for $N = 5$, of both genders. $N = 2$ reports rated as *low* in dissonance also reflected *no* shock, a religious preference of Protestant, were of married status with children, were involved in professional practice in medical institutional settings and were female; each of these N = 2 respondents saw the study's descriptive categorical terms of cognitive *dissonance* and cybernetic *shock* as either "negative" (cognitive dissonance) or "too dramatic" (shock). $N = 5$ understood cognitive dissonance as "apropos" or "a very good metaphor." Emergent emotional "labels" were noted as: stress, existential anxiety, panic, depression, alienation and/or loneliness.

Who or what helped you through this process?

Graduate student respondents (EVC) reported professors', colleagues' and professional personal supervision of cases as helpful. Meditation, a variety of "coping mechanisms," and comprehensive study groups were reported as helpful. $N = 2$ reported spousal support; the remainder ($N = 5$) related a provocative absence of close family members, friends, or co-therapists with whom they could talk. (Most respondents made and kept scheduled appointments for interviews even though on tight schedules during a busy December 1987 holiday season. They all expressed how they looked forward to discussing the "known" theme. They also expressed an interest in meeting later, as a group, to discuss the outcome of aggregate reports.)

What have been the ramifications involving your personal and professional life?

One respondent (EVC) reported "simple" systems thinking had enhanced communication with an adolescent family member, another as symmetrically conflicting with a spouse's views, a third and fourth that a cybernetic epistemology had improved interactions in their personal lives. None of the other ($N = 3$) respondents reported cybernetic epistemology as involved in enhancement of their interpersonal lives. All but one ($N = 6$) reported ramifications involving professional life with vivid reports of feeling as if they are "non-conformists." They shared heuristic "thick descriptions" of struggling with panic, stress, depression, loneliness, existential crises, and alienation.

What is the impact on your family and friends?

Again, respondent (EVC) reports indicate family members and friends as impacted in relation to intellectual and emotional responses of graduate students, which seemed to involve a deep awareness of an intellectual chasm, void, or gap developing between respondents and their families and friends. One respondent reported, "I have no friends . . . it's funny though that *may* have been possible—that's one thing that may have happened . . . don't seem to have much in common anymore." Another reported, "I don't want to talk about that." Others shared significant experiences related to others' views of their "new epistemology" as perceived as "my new Zen" or "my craziness."

What conclusions have you reached?

Overall (EVC) self-rating of the composite unity of dissonance/cybernetic epistemology/shock processes for $N=7$ ranged from 5 to 10; mode of 10; mean of 9 and/or as "Extremely Positive." In $N=2$ cases cognitive dissonance was rated as equally painful. Their words seem to say it best:

"It helps me."

"I'm grateful—I'm glad it happened—I wonder how long I would have gone on . . . if it hadn't been for [St. Louis University] SLU . . . I've become so aware . . . like a rebirth, a hatching or labor and delivery."

"I like it . . . kind of a moment of transcendence. Jumped a level of abstraction . . . then there's nothing there to jump to . . . it's very second order . . . or third order."

"I love to learn . . . new things and new ideas, new ways of seeing, it's exciting so that's positive. In terms of what Keeney says: it will forever change my life . . . I doubt it. . . ."

"It has been a way of getting more in touch with myself, causing me to examine and explore not only myself but my world, and it's caused me to look at everything differently—I mean *everything* socially, politically, etc . . . "

"We're getting to the place where we have limited natural resources, same of the economic difficulties . . . you know, maybe we're at a stage where we realize as much as we know, there's a lot we cannot control."

"I'm going to invent my own universe I think . . . (just kidding!)."

The foregoing represents the synthesis, in a patterned aggregate, of over ten hours of dialectic (120) pages of verbatim transcribed (EVC) responses, entered into by graduate students involved in higher level learning change. Much more is there than meets the eye. The essence involves an earlier transformation of Varela's quotation (cited in Keeney, 1983, p. 92):

Being Ph.D/is the process of becoming Ph.D., reflected in kind in the following, as Goodman (1978) reasoned, and Robertson (1987) cited, perhaps

> we do not begin with something absolute or prior to all reasoning . . . [we] begin instead with the kinds of construction

> that lead to the creation of worlds. And these constructions have in common that they take certain premises for granted, as stipulations. What is 'given' or assumed at the onset of our construction is neither bedrock reality out there, nor a priori: it is always another constructed version of a world that we have taken as given for certain purposes. Any previously constructed world version may be taken as given for subsequent construction. So, in effect, world making involves the transformation of worlds and world versions already made.
>
> [p. 455]

(from Jerome Bruner's *Actual Minds, Possible Worlds,* Cambridge: Harvard Univ. Press, 1986)

The study/inquiry illuminates patterns that connect the change of world view theme for these Ph.D. students. The expressed verbal content (EVC) in interviews seems to involve only minor variance, with the hypothesized pattern involved in the duration and degree of cognitive dissonance and cybernetic shock experienced and described in the study. Introduction to the "dynamic web of interrelated events" perturbs the processes of becoming a cybernetic epistemologist. Above all, these graduate students seemed to embrace a Bootstrapper's approach consonant with an L. III approach (Chew, Capra, 1983). Graduate students seemed "able to view any number of different partially successful models or patterns without favoritism." They re-cognized that "patterns do not 'contain' one another but rather 'involve' one another" (pp. 94–95).

Graduate students, in the process of becoming cybernetic epistemologists, get used to knowing tricks of a cybernetic epistemology. The content (EVC) of their responses reflected their *becoming* involvement. They immerse themselves in the primary meta process of a cybernetic epistemology, re-cognizing epistemological patterns of linearity, circularity, meta-recursion, self-reference, paradox, autonomy, the sacred and chaotic. They conduct their own meta-research, responsibly exploring uncharted (sometimes dangerous and chaotic) levels of recursion—i.e., *left-handed complimentarity*. Their patterned processes of re-constructed versions and visions fit Bateson's Logical Levels of Learning change. A cybernetic epistemology is L. III process of change of world view.

In graduate or at any level of education "the difference that makes a difference . . . is 'INFORMATION' " (Bateson, 1979, p. 68). Information perturbs "what we know . . . when the body of knowledge changes, so do we" (Burke, 1979, p. 11). A recent editorial by Washington correspondent William Safire touched on the urgency of sacred higher levels of knowledge change. In it he attacked the level of sacredness of Pope John Paul II and "his 20,000-word personally written encyclical, 'The Social Concerns of the Church' . . . [commenting] He is about a decade behind in geopolitics." This journalistic attack was based on direct quotes taken from Pope John Paul II's encyclical. Cited was " 'the existence of *two opposing* blocs . . . two very different *visions* of man and of his freedom and social role.' " Safire wrote "the official *world view* of the Vatican . . . is *wronghanded*." He implied that his own choice of world view is *bound* to *"John Locke"* (italics added), (1988, February 25, *St. Louis Post-Dispatch,* Editorial, p. 3B). (The meta–double-bind of either/or recursive processes turns and recircles—as the author feared.) Clearly, cybernetic epistemological change lies even beyond what some consider the sacred patterns of either/or dissonant META double-binds. Epistemological change lies beyond traditional and residual framed metaphors depicting any dynamic of "Revolutions as Change of World View" (Kuhn, 1962, 1970, pp. 111–135). Universal change of epistemology most certainly lies beyond the grasp of any and all who, caught up in meta patterns of dissonance, "speak and do not know," or, in shock, "know but do not speak" (Bateson & Bateson, 1987, p. 10). While the author and respondents did fit a Kuhnian description of graduate students "at the cutting edge" of inventive change, "youthfulness" is no longer part of the "new look" of higher education. Respondents' ages (mean = 36) and the additional "shift" of gender balance, twice as many females' reflect new patterns of mature graduate/undergraduate students. All respondents were enrolled on a part-time basis, practiced both full and/or part time, and had financial-aid commitments (with pay-back beginning six months after graduation). The "new face" of education is sharply reflected in these graduate student respondents revising traditional/residual concepts of the current makeup of education. This dissertation speaks to those present and future "mature, responsible, non-conformist, Bootstrappers out there!"

This dissertation neither reached for conclusions nor sought to resolve problems. Heuristically, it records what is, as it is, and chronicles patterns that connect cybernetic epistemology to processes of higher learning level change . . . of world view . . . *Beyond Revolutions* . . . as change.

APPENDIXES

Appendix A
Consent for Participation in Research Activities

June DiSalvo, M.S.W., has requested my participation in a study being conducted as part of her doctoral research at St. Louis University. The study is: On Becoming a Cybernetic Epistemologist: A Heuristic Inquiry Into Student Intellectual and Emotional Response to Their Introduction to Cybernetic Epistemology in the Major Area of Individual, Marriage & Family development & Therapy of Counseling Education at St. Louis University. I understand that the purpose of the research is to investigate the experience of being a doctoral student in the Individual, Marriage & Family Development & Therapy program.

My participation will involve a single private general interview lasting 90 minutes, conducted by the researcher. I understand that this session will be tape recorded.

As a respondent my contribution to the data will be summarized with other respondents and my identity will be known only by the researcher.

I understand there are no risks involved other than those which may be involved with increased self-awareness. Confidentiality and anonymity will be protected by the researcher according to ethical guidelines set forth in the Ethical Principles of the American Psychological Association, and the Code of the National Association of Social Workers, of which the researcher is a member. Further, I understand that if side effects or discomforts do occur, I may contact June DiSalvo, and that if she is unable to assist me personally she will make an appropriate referral.

I understand that the results of the research may be published but that my name and identity will not be revealed and that my records will remain confidential. In order that confidentiality can be maintained, June DiSalvo will remain bound by her professional code of ethics. Names and direct references to me will be omitted.

I understand that my participation in this study will not benefit me. I understand that providing information and insights of a subjective nature may serve to guide further research and inquiry and increase our stores of knowledge as a potential benefit to society.

I understand that one alternative is nonparticipation.

I also understand that my participation is voluntary and that refusal to participate will involve no penalty to me or loss of benefits to which I am otherwise entitled. I also understand that I may withdraw from the research study at any time without penalty or prejudice.

Any questions that I may have concerning my participation in the research study or my rights as a research subject will be answered by June DiSalvo.

I understand that the University will provide immediate treatment in the event that an injury results because of my participation in this project. I also understand that no financial compensation will be paid to me by the University.

In the event I believe I have suffered any injury as a result of participation in the research project, I am to contact the Chairman of the St. Louis University Institutional Review Board (577-8108), who will be able to refer me to the individual who will review the matter with me, identify other resources that may be available to me, and provide further information as to how to proceed.

I have read the above statement and have been able to ask questions and express concerns which have been satisfactorily responded to by the investigator. I believe I understand the purpose of the study as well as the potential benefits and risks that are involved. I hereby give my informed and free consent to be a participant in this study.

____________________ Date   ______________________________

Signature of Subject

SLU INSTITUTIONAL REVIEW BOARD
Approved yes
Date 6/18/87

I certify that I have explained to the above individual the nature and purpose, the potential benefits and possible risks associated with participation in this research study, have answered any questions that have been raised, and have witnessed the above signature.

The elements of informed consent conform to the assurance given by Saint Louis University to the DHHS to protect the rights of human subjects.

I have provided the subject a copy of this signed consent document.

____________ Date   ______________________________

Signature of Investigator
(Must be signed at the time of consent.)

APPENDIX B

Request for Volunteers for Participation in Dissertation Research

WHO?	For self-selected doctoral residents in their last semester in Individual, Marriage & Family Development & Therapy. Conducted by June DiSalvo, M.S.W., in conjunction with dissertation research for the Ph.D. in Education with a Major in Individual, Marriage & Family Development & Therapy.
WHAT?	An experiential study of students in Individual, Marriage & Family Development and Therapy, consisting of one 90 minute private interview with the researcher. TOPIC: On Becoming a Cybernetic Epistemologist: A Heuristic Inquiry Into Student Intellectual & Emotional Response to Their Introduction to Cybernetic Epistemology in the Major Area of Individual, Marriage & Family Development & Therapy of Counseling Education at St. Louis University.
WHEN?	Focused interview arranged at time convenient for volunteer.
WHERE?	Arranged at the convenience of the volunteer.
WHY?	Respondents provide information and insights of a subjective nature, to be summarized and included in a dissertation, which may guide further research and inquiry and increase our stores of knowledge to benefit society.
HOW?	Focused interview regarding the experience of being a doctoral student with a major in Individual, Marriage & Family Development and Therapy.

APPENDIX C
Focused Interview Schedule

For a number of years you have been involved in your doctoral studies in Individual, Marriage and Family Development and Therapy. In the course of your studies there may have occurred a change in your thinking.

The purpose of this interview is to discuss your subjective experience of: Becoming a Cybernetic Epistemologist: A Heuristic Inquiry Into Student Intellectual and Emotional Response to Their Introduction to Cybernetic Epistemology in the Major Area of Individual, Marriage & Family Development & Therapy of Counseling Education at St. Louis University. The questions generally focus on:

How have you experienced this process?
Who or what helped you through this process?
What have been the ramifications involving your personal and professional life?
What is the impact on your family and friends?
What conclusions have you reached?

After discussing these 5 questions I would be intensely interested in any other experiences you consider will contribute to the validity/reliability of this heuristic inquiry of the doctoral students' experiences in this major area.

All reporting of responses will be in aggregates in the form of patterns, categories and themes which characterize this process.

Glossary

AESTHETIC Bateson (1979): "I mean responsive to the pattern which connects" (p. 8). Keeney (1983) quoted Bateson proposing "that the patterns that bind ideas together 'are as close as we can get to ultimate truth.' The dances between form and process, skeletons of symbolic relations and sensory based description, letter and spirit, rigor and imagination represent . . . 'dialectical necessities of the living world.' It is here that we encounter the aesthetics of change . . . representing a hierarchy of orders of recursion. None of these orders—action, context, and metacontext—is actually lower or higher than any of the others in spatial sense; such distribution is an artifact" (pp. 46–47). Furthermore, Keeney (1983) related his [aesthetic] "position is to avoid any type of either/or dichotomy . . . prefer[ring] to view aesthetics [responsiveness to the patterns which connect] as a contextual frame for practical action" (p. 8). *See also* Patterns That Connect, Recursion and Draw a Distinction.
COMPLEMENTARY Bateson (1979): "by contrast to symmetry—A and B actions [are] different but mutually fitted each other e.g., dominance-submission, exhibition-spectatorship, dependence-nurturance." Becvar and Becvar (1982): "Interaction between . . . is characterized by a high frequency of exchanges of opposite kinds of behavior" (p. 23). *See also* Symmetry and Draw a Distinction.
CYBERNETICS "[from Gr. kybernetes, helmsman . . .] the comparative study of the human nervous system and of complex electronic calculating machines, aimed at increasing the understanding of how the human brain functions" (*Webster's*, 2 ed., 1983). "A branch of mathematics dealing with problems of control, recursiveness, and information" (Bateson, 1979, p. 227). The science of patterns of organizational structure. *See* Cybernetic Complementarity and epistemology.
CYBERNETIC COMPLEMENTARITY Keeney (1983) related "involves different orders of recursion, which demonstrate how 'pairs (poles, extremes, modes, sides) are related and yet remain distinct' . . . Cybernetic complementarities provide a way of encapsulating the recursive nature of natural epistemology, i.e., an alternative framework for examining distinctions; Varela's formula, 'the it'/'the

process leading to it.' For the most part, people take distinction to be either/or duality, a polarity, a clash of opposites (A/not A; right/wrong; useful/not useful; bad/good) . . . we speak of winning or losing in a zero-sum fashion" (p. 92). "Sometimes, however, people draw distinctions meant to indicate a pair of opposites with each side belonging to the same order of process, i.e., the pair 'predator/prey' is sometimes proposed as operating in terms of excluding opposites . . . a dualism (Varela calls) a 'hegelian pair,' . . . [this] is an incomplete sketch . . . Varela requires we see these as one side of a larger cybernetic complementarity, 'For every pair A/not A, there exists a more inclusive [form], where the apparent opposites are components of more encompassing cybernetic complementarity, i.e., the battle over food and territory between two species is only one half of the story . . . the larger picture is that the battle is a means or process of generating, maintaining and stabilizing an ecosystem." (pp. 93–194). See also: Left-handed Compliment.

CYBERNETIC EPISTEMOLOGY Keeney (1983): "a process of knowing constructing and maintaining a world of experience" (pp. 107–108). Keeney (1983): "specifying the meaning of cybernetic epistemology . . . we are, at best, in a state of epistemological transition—that few, if any, individuals are habitually experiencing their world through cybernetic epistemology . . . we are so accustomed to noncybernetic ways of knowing that we may distort whatever glimpse of cybernetics might fall our way . . . we may forget that our creative imagination is free to draw distinctions. Cybernetic epistemology provides a way of discovering and constructing alternative patterns in the ecology of our experience [p. 48]. The trick is to re-cognize patterns [p. 60]. The identity of living process with mental process . . . Mind and nature become an inseparable unity . . . part of a more encompassing ecological dance . . . [p. 108] . . . a jump from the paradigm of substance to that of pattern . . . can embody the complementary gestalt of simple cybernetics and cybernetics of cybernetics . . . able to jump back and forth between those orders of recursion. . . . With this full view, [one] can approach the complexity and elegance of autonomous and interconnected patterns of life" (p. 109). Segal (1986): "von Foerster with his cybernetic ideas of memory . . . circular causal feedback mechanisms in biological and social systems" (p. 158).

CYBERNETICS OF CYBERNETICS Margaret Mead (1968), in Keeney (1983), held: "[Cybernetics of cybernetics] [is a] way of pointing to the observer's inclusion and participation in the system. [It] jumps an order of recursion and places the observer as part of the observed. . . ." [p. 76].

What von Foerster called 'second order cybernetics' places the observer in that which is observed, all description is self-referential [p. 77]. . . . [We are] free to carve the world as we like as long as our carvings are remembered to be approximations of the more encompassing recursive patterns from which they are demarcated. Simple cybernetics and cybernetics of cybernetics are halves of a cybernetic complementarity" (p. 101). See also: Recursion, Self-reference and Paradox.

DOUBLE-BIND Webster's (1983, 2nd Ed.): "1. a situation in which a person is faced with contradictory demands, expectations, etc. so that any action taken will appear to be wrong. 2. any dilemma (sense 2)." You're damned if you do—and damned if you don't. *See also* Paradox.

DRAW A DISTINCTION Segal (1986) cited Keeney: " 'The most basic act of epistemology is to create a distinction. It is only by distinguishing one pattern from another that we are able to know our world ' " (p. 61). Keeney (1983) cites, "in the beginning G. Spencer-Brown insisted: 'Draw a distinction!' . . . whether obeyed consciously or unconsciously, is the starting point for any action, decision, perception, thought, description, theory, and epistemology . . . 'the boundaries can be drawn anywhere we please' thus, an infinitude of universes are possible from the primordial creative act of drawing distinctions" (p. 18). Further, "dealing within our distinction between sensory based description and skeletons of symbolic relations is the recursive operation of an observer drawing a distinction. Tracing this recursive operation of drawing distinctions, distinctions upon distinctions and so on, enables us to uncover the way we construct and bind together an ecology of ideas—the construction and maintenance of a reality" (p. 46). *See also* Patterns That Connect, Recursion, Self-reference and Paradox, and Cybernetic Complementarity.

EPISTEMOLOGY Bateson (1979): "A branch of science combined with a branch of philosophy. As science, epistemology is the study of how particular organisms or aggregates of organisms know, think and decide. As philosophy, epistemology is the study of necessary limits and other characteristics of the processes of knowing, thinking and deciding." Webster's (1983, 2ed.): "[Gr. episteme, knowledge, and logos, discourse] the theory or science that investigates the origin, nature, methods, and limits of knowledge." *See also* Cybernetics and Cybernetic Epistemology.

EVOLUTIONARY CUL-DE-SAC Bateson (1979): "Tennyson says, 'lest one good custom should corrupt the world.' There are subcycles of living and dying within the bigger, more enduring ecology. But what shall we say of the death of the larger system? Any species can get into an evolutionary cu-de-sac, and I suppose it is a mistake of sorts for that species to be a party to its own extinction. The human species, as we all know, may extinguish itself any day now" (p. 208). *See also* Game without End.

GAME WITHOUT END "A system which may run through all its possible internal changes (no matter how many there are) without effecting a systemic change, i.e., second-order change, is said to be caught in a Game Without End. It cannot generate from within itself the conditions for its own change; it cannot produce the rules for the change of its own rules . . . They are endless in the sense that they contain no provisions for their own termination . . . Termination (like waking up, in our nightmare . . .) is not part of the game, it is not a member of that group; termination is meta to the game, is of a different logical type than any move (any first-order change) within the game" (Watzlawick, et. al, 1974, p. 22).

LEFT-HANDED COMPLIMENT Questionable, "insincere or dubious complimentary expression. . . . COMPLEMENT: 2. to compli*i*-ment. [Obs.]" (*Webster's* (1983, 2 ed.).

META *Webster's* (1983, 2 ed.): "[Gr. meta-, from prep. meta, in the midst of among, between, after, according to.] 1. changed in position or form, altered, transposed, as in metamorphosis, metathesis; equivalent to trans-. 2. after, as in metaphysics; sometimes, as in medical terms, equivalent to post-. 4. [from supposed analogy to metaphysics] beyond, higher, transcending . . . " (Hierarchical definitions are considered by the references in this study/inquiry "artifacts" of our habitual ways of drawing distinctions and punctuating, i.e., patterns "involve" one another.)

META–DOUBLE-BIND "One is trapped between two unacceptable alternatives which can be stated explicitly (double-bind). In a meta double-bind the individual is bound to a frame of reference in which the solution cannot be described because it lies outside the frame of reference being used" (Weeks and L'Abate, 1982, p. 43). *See also* Paradox (either/or thinking pattern).

PARADOX Webster (1983, 2 ed.): "[Fr. paradoxe; Gr. paradoxon; para, beyond, and doxon, opinion; dokein, to think or suppose.] 1. a statement contrary to common belief. [Rare.] 2. a statement that seems contradictory, unbelievable, or absurd but that may actually be true in fact. 3. a statement that is self-contradictory in fact and, hence, false. 4. (a) something inconsistent with common experience or having contradictory qualities; (b) a person who is inconsistent or contradictory in character or behavior. Syn.—contradiction, enigma, mystery, absurdity, ambiguity." *See also* Double-bind.

PATTERNS THAT CONNECT Keeney (1983) said: "Orienting ourselves toward seeing 'patterns that connect' leads us to experiencing an aesthetics of our ecosystem" (p. 139). Examples: Lineal; circular; recursive; binocular vision; versus and verses; transient therapeutic triangulation, et. al. Bateson (1979) explained the " 'pattern is a metapattern, pattern of patterns . . . 1st order connections, 2nd order connections, 3rd order connections" (p. 8).

Becvar and Becvar (1982) wrote of "a reciprocal or circular notion of causality. A and B are in dynamic interaction:

(p. 7). *Also see* Cybernetic complementarity, Cybernetics of cybernetics and Recursion.

PHYSICAL METAPHORS Habitually, "used to describe and explain mental phenomena, power, tension, energy, social forces. Recursive natural epistemology—cybernetic complementarity involves different order of recursion, which demonstrate how 'pairs (poles, extremes, modes, sides) are related and yet remain distinct.' (Cybernetic complementarities proved a way of encapsulating the recursive nature of natural epistemology.)" (Keeney, 1983, p. 91.) "Revolutions as Changes of World View" (Kuhn, 1962, 1970, pp. 111–35). "Power" metaphors —conflict paradigm.

PUNCTUATION The "punctuation of a sequence of events . . . is analogous to the concept of indication—an observer draws a distinction concomitantly makes an indication—he marks one of the two distinguished sides as being primary, i.e., 'this,' 'I,' 'us,' . . . It is the very purpose of the distinction to create this indication. The use of distinction to create indication is a way of defining punctuation." Further, "peoples' punctuation of their experience identifies their epistemology. Their habitual patterns of punctuation presuppose epistemological premises for making distinctions . . . one's epistemological 'slip' is always showing" (Keeney, 1983, p. 25). Recursive order "meta" to the drawing of a distinction. *See also* Draw a Distinction and Epistemology.

RECIPROCAL Webster's (1983, 2 ed.): "1. anything that has a reciprocal action on or relation to another; a complement, counterpart, equivalent, etc." *See also* Patterns That Connect.

RECURSION (AND ORDERS OF): Webster's (1983, 2 ed.): "return (Obs.)." Keeney (1983) summed up a "Hierarchy of logical levels, recursively structured, i.e., page, is a part of chapter, part of a book, book is a part of a encyclopedia . . . distinctions drawn on distinction . . . i.e., member, frame, metaframe. . . . Like the Ouroborous—mythical creature—the snake that eats its own tail . . . Each time it swallows itself, the creation of a different order of recursion—episodes of infolding—recognize a difference each time the circle travels through itself . . . [as] indicating an order of recycling— [can] mark the order of recursion invoked in any given description/explanation [p. 32]. [Not] representing a hierarchy of orders of recursion. None of these orders—action, context, and metacontext—is actually lower or higher than any of the others in spatial sense; such distribution is an artifact" (pp. 46—47). Hofstader (1979) called recursion "Strange Loopiness" (p. 21). *See also* Cybernetic complementarity; Patterns That Connect; Symmetry; Complementary; Self-reference and Paradox.

SYMMETRY Bateson (1979): "typology of process—all forms of interaction that can be described as competition, rivalry, mutual emulation, and so on (i.e., those in which A's action of a given kind would stimulate B to action of the same kind, which in turn would stimulate A to further similar actions, and so on. If A boasts— B furthers boasting & vice versa)" (p. 105). Becvar and Becvar (1982): . . . "the interaction between . . . is characterized by a high frequency of the same kinds of behavior" (p. 23). One-upmanship—the nuclear arms race. *See also* Complementary and Patterns That Connect.

SCHISMOGENESIS Bateson (1979): "As a matter of history, systems with positive gain, variously called escalating or vicious circles . . . [are] characterized by interchanges of behavior such that the more A exhibited a given behavior the more B was likely to exhibit the same [symmetrical interchanges]; interchanges in which B's behavior was different from but complementary to that of A [complementary interchanges]; in either case, the relations were potentially subject to progressive escalation—called 'schismogenic' " (p. 105). *See also* Complementary Symmetry, Recursion, and Patterns That Connect, Left-handed compliment.

SELF-HEALING TAUTOLOGY Bateson (1979) held: "the world of mental process is both tautological and ecological. I mean that it is a slowly self-healing tautology. Left to itself, any large piece . . . will tend to settle toward tautology, that is, toward internal consistency of ideas and processes. But every now and then, the consistency gets torn; the tautology breaks up like the surface of a pond when a stone is thrown into it. Then the tautology slowly but immediately starts to heal. And the healing may be ruthless . . . whole species may be wiped out" (p. 206). *Also see* Game Without End.

SELF-REFERENCE AND PARADOX Keeney (1983) terms as " 'Errors of Objectivity.' Since cybernetics of cybernetics, or what von

Foerster calls 'second cybernetics,' places the observer in that which is observed, all description is self-referential. [A] 1901 Theory of Logical Types was an attempt to avoid any contradictions and self-referential paradoxes . . . Godel (1931) proved that there is no way of getting rid of the self-referential paradoxical beasts which are a natural part of any formal system of thinking . . . von Foerster: 'Self-reference' in scientific discourse was always though to be illegitimate, for it was generally believed that The Scientific Method rests on 'objective' statements that are supposedly observer-independent. . . . This belief is unfounded . . . as shown by John von Neuman, Gotthard, Gunther, Lars Lofgren and many others" (p. 78).

Bibliography

Allender, J. S. (1986). Educational research: A personal and social process. *Review of Educational Research, 56*(2), 173–193.

Auger, L. (1987). Can humans think their way to increased freedom. *Journal of RET, 5*(1), 54–58.

Babbie, E. (1983). *The practice of social research.* 3d ed. Belmont: Wadsworth.

Bateson, G. (1972). *Steps to an ecology of mind. A Revolutionary approach to man's understanding of himself.* New York: Harper & Row. Reprinted by permission of publisher.

*Bateson, G. (1979). *Mind and Nature: A necessary unity.* New York: Dutton.

Bateson, M.C. (1985). We are the world, we are the parents: Together we give birth to the future. *The Family Therapy Networker, 9*(5), 42–45.

Becvar, D. S. (Spring 1986). Class notes. Advanced individual, marriage & family therapy (ED145-665). Department of Education: St. Louis University at St. Louis.

Becvar, R. (Spring 1985). Class notes. Human development ecology (ED145-673). Department of Education: St. Louis University of St. Louis.

Becvar, R. J., and Becvar, D. S. (1982). *Systems theory and family therapy, a primer.* Washington, D.C.: University Press.

Bloom, A. (1987). *The closing of the American mind: How higher education has failed democracy and impoverished the souls of today's students.* New York: Simon and Schuster.

Bredo, E. (1987). Bateson's communicative approach to learning. Presented at 1987 meeting of AESA. Chicago. (11/4–5/87.)

*Briggs, J. P., and Peat, F. D. (1984). *Looking glass universe: The emerging science of wholeness* New York: Simon and Schuster.

Broderick, C. (1983). *The therapeutic triangle.* Beverly Hills: Sage Publications.

*Bronowski, J. (1978). *The origins of knowledge and imagination.* New Haven and London: Yale University Press.

Broudy, Harry S. "The life uses of schooling as a field for research," in *Philosophical redirection of educational research,* ed. L. G. Thomas, Seventy-first Yearbook of the National Society for the Study of Education, Part 1 (Chicago: University of Chicago Press, 1972).

Burke, J. (1985). *The day the universe changed.* Boston: Little, Brown and Company.

Calapinto, J. (1985). Maturana and the ideology of conformity. *The Family Therapy Networker, 9*(3), 29–30.

Capra, F. (1984). *The tao of physics.* New York: Bantam Books.

Davis, P. J., and Hersh, R. (1986). *Descartes' dream: the world according to mathematics*. New York: Harcourt Brace Jovanovich.

Dell, P. F. (1985). Understanding Bateson and Maturana: Toward a biological foundation for the social sciences. *Journal of Marital & Family Therapy, 11*(1), 1–20.

Douglas, J. (1976) *Investigative social research*. Beverly Hills: Sage Pub.

Douglass, B. G., and Moustakas, C. (1985). Heuristic inquiry: The internal search to know. *Journal of Humanistic Psychology, 25*(3), 39–55.

Durant, W. (1953). *The story of philosophy*. New York: Simon and Schuster.

Efram, J. S., and Lukens, J. J. (1985). The world according to Humberto Maturana. *The Family Therapy Networker, 9*(3), 22–28.

Efram, J. S., and Lukens, J. J. (1986). The quest for causes: What the constructivists are saying about us these days. *The Family Therapy Networker, 10*(6), 65–67.

Ellis, A., and Harper, R. A. (1975). *A new guide to rational living*. Hollywood: Wilshire Book Co.

Evans, J. A. S. (1982). *Herodotus*. Boston: Twane.

Feigenbaum, J. J. (1987, July 8). Study of chaos. *St. Louis Post-Dispatch*, p. 4.

*Ferguson, M. (1980). *The Aquarian conspiracy: Personal and social transformation in the 1980's*. New York: St. Martins Press.

Festinger, L. (1957). *A theory of cognitive dissonance*. Stanford, CI.: Stanford University Press.

Ford, J. (1975). *Paradigms and fairy tales: An introduction to the science of meanings*. 2 vol. London and Boston: Routledge and Kegan.

Foucault, M. (1973). *The order of things: An archaeology of the human sciences*. New York: Vantage Books.

Fraser, J. C., (1984). Process level integration: Corrective vision for a binocular view. *The Journal of Strategic & Systemic Therapies, 3*(3 & 4), 43.

Futtermann, E. (1988, February 1). Mispronunciations. *St. Louis Post-Dispatch*, pp. 1, 8.

Gleick, J. (1987). *Chaos: Making a new science*. New York: Viking Press.

Gleick, J. (1987). New images of chaos that are stirring a science revolution. *Smithsonian, 18*(9), 122.

Godley, A. D. (1960). *Herodotus*. Translation, Vol. 1, 2, 3, 4. Cambridge and London: Harvard Press.

Gowin, D. Bob. "Is educational research distinctive?" in *Philosophical redi*rection of educational research, ed. L. G. Thomas, Seventy-first Yearbook of the National Society for the Study of Education, Part I (Chicago: University of Chicago Press, 1972).

Guerin, P. (ed.) (1976). *Family therapy: Theory and practice*. New York: Gardner Press.

Gurman, A. (1983). The old hatters and the new wavers. *The Family Therapy Networker, 7*(4), 37.

*Hampden-Turner, C. (1981). *Maps of the mind*. New York: Macmillan Publishing.

Hannon, J. (1986). Thine is the power, an epistemological fable. *The Family Therapy Networker, 10*(4), 49–51.
*Hesse, H. (1969). *Magister Ludi: The glass bead game.* New York: Bantam Books.
Hoffman, L. (1981). *Foundations of family therapy.* New York: Basic Books.
Hofstadter, D. R. (1979). *Godel, Escher, Bach: An eternal golden braid.* New York: Basic Books.
Hollenbach, D. R. (1970). *Claims in conflict.* New York: Paulist Press.
Jahoda, M., Deutsch, M., and Cook, S. W. (1951). *Research methods in social relations* Part 1: Basic Processes. New York: Dryden Press.
Jantsch, E. (1980). *The self-organizing universe: Scientific and human implications of the emerging paradigm of evolution.* Oxford: Pergamon Press.
Jones, J., and Wilson, W. (1987). *An incomplete education.* New York: Ballantine Books.
Jowett, B. (1946). *Plato, The republic.* Translation. Cleveland and New York: World Publishing.
Keeney, B. P. (1983). *Aesthetics of change.* New York: Guilford Press.
Keeney, B., and Ross, J. (1985). The dance of duality. *The Family Therapy Networker, 9*(3), 46–50.
Kirk, J., and Miller, M. (1986). *Reliability and validity in qualitative research.* Qualitative Research Methods Series, volume 1. Beverly Hills: Sage Pub.
Kniskern, D. P. (1983). The new wave is all wet. . . . *The Family Therapy Networker, 7*(4), 38, 61–62.
Kuhn, T. S. (1962). *The structure of scientific revolutions.* Chicago: University of Chicago Press, *11(2).*
**Kuhn, T. S. (1970). The structure of scientific revolutions,* Second Enlarged edition. Chicago: University of Chicago Press.
Laing, R. D. (1964). Mystification, confusion, and conflict. *Intensive Family Therapy,* unreferenced chapter, 343–363.
MacKinnon, L. D., and Slive, A. (1984). If one should not marry a hypothesis, should one marry a model? *Journal of Strategic and Systemic Therapies, 3*(4), 26–39.
Macmillian, C. J. B., and Garrison, J. W. (1984). Using the "new philosophy of science" in criticizing current research traditions in education. *Educational Review, 13*(10), 15–21.
May, R. (1969). *Love and will.* Introduction: Our schizoid world. New York: W. W. Norton. 14–33.
Morowitz, H. J. (1985). *Mayonnaise and the origins of life: Thoughts of minds and molecules.* New York: Charles Scribner's & Sons.
Nunner-Winkler, G. (1984). Two moralities? A critical discussion of ethic of care & responsibility versus an ethic of rights and justice. Chapter 19, *Of Virtue & Imperfect Duties.* New York: John Wiley.
Palazzoli, M. S. (1978). The tyranny of linguistic conditioning. *Paradox and Counterparadox,* Chapter 6. New York: Aronson. 51–66.
Patton, M. C. (1980). *Qualitative evaluation methods.* Beverly Hills: Sage Publications.

Popkewitz, T. S. (1984). *Paradigm and ideology in educational research.* London and New York: Falmer Press.

Reynolds, P. (1971). *A primer in theory construction.* Indianapolis: Bobbs-Merrill.

Robertson, R. (1987). Omnibus review. *Psychological Perspectives, 18*(2), 455; quoting from Bruner, Jerome (1986), Actual minds, Possible Worlds.

Rosenthal. P. (1984). *Words and values.* New York: Oxford Press.

Rychlak, Joseph F. (1981). *Introduction to personality and psychotherapy: A theory construction approach,* Second Edition. Copyright © 1981 by Houghton Mifflin Company. Paraphrased with permission.

St. Louis Post-Dispatch (1987, May 24), editorial commentary, p. 3.

Scarf, M. (1987). *Intimate partners, patterns in love and marriage.* New York: Random House.

Schatzman, L., and Strauss, A. L. (1973). *Field research: Strategies for a natural sociology.* Englewood Cliffs, N.J.: Prentice-Hall.

Schwartz, R. C., and Breunlin, D. (1983). Research: Why clinicians should bother with it. . . . *The Family Therapy Networker, 7*(4), 24–27, 57–59.

Segal, L. (1986). *The dream of reality: Heinz von Foerster's constructivism.* New York: W. W. Norton.

Simon, R. (1985). Structure is destiny: An interview with Humberto Maturana. *The Family Therapy Networker, 9*(3), 32–43.

Sluzki, C. E. (1985). A minimal map of cybernetics. *The Family Therapy Networker, 9*(3), 26.

Stern, K. (1972). *The flight from woman.* New York: Noonday Press.

Thomas, L. G., Ed. *Philosophical redirection of educational research.* Seventy-first Yearbook of the National Society for the Study of Education, Part 1 (Chicago: University of Chicago Press, 1972).

Toffler, A. (1970) *Future shock.* New York: Bantam.

Toffler, A. (1980) *The third wave.* New York: Bantam.

Tomm, K. (1983). The old hat doesn't fit. *The Family Therapy Networker, 7*(4), 39–40.

Trefil, T. (1987). Quantum physics' world: now you see it, now you don't. *Smithsonian, 18*(5), 66–75.

Wagenaar, T. C., and Babbie E. (1983). *Practicing social research,* Third Edition. Guided activities to accompany the practice of social research. Belmont, CI.: Wadsworth.

Watzlawick, P., Beavin, J., and Jackson, D. (1967). *Pragmatics of human communication.* New York and London: Norton.

Watzlawick, P., Weakland, J., and Fisch, R. (1974). *Change: Principles of problem formation and problem resolution.* New York: W. W. Norton.

Weeks, G., and L'Abate, L. (1982). *Paradoxical psychotherapy theory & practice with individuals, couples & families.* New York: Brunner/Mazel.

Whitaker, C. (1972). The hindrance of theory in clinical work. Unreferenced article. 154–164.

Whitaker, C. (1975). Psychotherapy of the absurd: With a special emphasis on the psychotherapy of aggression. *Family Process, 14*(1), 1–15.